LEADERS OF THE CIVIL WAR ERA

Harriet Tubman

LEADERS OF THE CIVIL WAR ERA

John Brown

Jefferson Davis

Frederick Douglass

Ulysses S. Grant

Stonewall Jackson

Robert E. Lee

Abraham Lincoln

William Tecumseh Sherman

Harriet Beecher Stowe

Harriet Tubman

LEADERS OF THE CIVIL WAR ERA

Harriet Tubman

WITHDRAWN

Ann Malaspina

CHELSEA HOUSE
PUBLISHERS
An imprint of Infobase Publishing

HARRIET TUBMAN

Chelsea House
An imprint of Infobase Publishing
132 West 31st Street
New York NY 10001

Library of Congress Cataloging-in-Publication Data
Malaspina, Ann, 1957-
Harriet Tubman / Ann Malaspina.
    p. cm. — (Leaders of the Civil War era)
Includes bibliographical references and index.
ISBN 978-1-60413-303-5 (hardcover)
1. Tubman, Harriet, 1820?-1913—Juvenile literature. 2. Slaves—United States—
Biography—Juvenile literature. 3. African American women—Biography—Juvenile
literature. 4. Underground Railroad—Juvenile literature. I. Title. II. Series.
E444.T82M343 2009
973.7'115—dc22
[B]   2008042412

Series design by Erik Lindstrom
Cover design by Keith Trego

Printed in the United States of America

Bang KT 10 9 8 7 6 5 4 3 2 1

This book is printed on acid-free paper.

CONTENTS

"No Sweet, No Sugar"

No one recorded the date on which a baby named Araminta Ross was born, in a slave cabin on the Eastern Shore of Maryland, sometime about 1820. Araminta, who was nicknamed "Minty," was a middle child of Harriet Green and Ben Ross, a slave couple on a timber plantation in Dorchester County. Most likely, none of their children, who numbered nine in all, had birth certificates. Slave owners did not mark the births of slaves, who were considered property, not people. Araminta's parents kept no written record of her birth because they did not know how to read or write.

Araminta Ross grew up to become Harriet Tubman, one of history's most admired and respected women. Her refusal to accept the sufferings and humiliations of a life of slavery guided her life's story. She accomplished the unbelievable. She not only saved herself from a life in bondage, but also risked grave danger to lead dozens of people along the Underground Railroad. That so-called "railroad" was a network of white and African-American volunteers who helped slaves escape to freedom in northern states or Canada.

Just as the date of Harriet Tubman's birth remains unknown—she told people that she was born in 1825, but her gravestone reads 1820—much of her life is wrapped in mystery. Because Tubman, like most American slaves, was never taught to read or write, she was unable to write her autobiography. Before the 1960s, what people knew about her life remained vague; her story seemed to be more folktale than biography. Although there were picture books written and stories told about the woman known as the "Moses of Her People," the world still wondered about the real Tubman.

In the early 2000s, historians and writers dug through slave records and other primary source documents such as newspaper columns and reward posters for runaway slaves. The researchers interviewed Tubman's present-day relatives and examined the writings of people who knew her and others who lived in her time. The historians put together a clearer picture of Tubman's long, eventful life. Her biography, as it has emerged in more detail, is no less amazing than the versions told in children's folktales. Tubman was not only a "conductor" on the Underground Railroad. She was also a loving daughter, sister, and wife; a nurse and a spy during the American Civil War; and a fundraiser for the antislavery movement. She also was a suffragist, a fighter for the rights of women, particularly African-American women, long after America's slaves won their freedom.

A famous photograph of Tubman in her later years shows a small woman with a strong face and determined eyes. Photographs do not reveal, however, that she was said to have had a lovely singing voice. She also told wonderful stories and liked to laugh. Her religious faith was deep, and it carried her through terrible hardships. Tubman's exuberant sense of hope

Harriet Tubman, born Araminta Ross (c. 1820–1913), was one of nine children born to slave parents. Although born into a system where there was no hope, Tubman escaped slavery and became an abolitionist, humanitarian, Union spy and nurse, and the rescuer of more than 70 slaves using a network of anti-slavery activists and safe houses known as the Underground Railroad.

and her steely determination led her far away from her slavery roots, but that memorable journey came later. Before anything else, she had to survive her childhood, a time during which her fate, like that of her parents and grandparents before her, seemed sealed.

BORN INTO SLAVERY

Little is known about Tubman's ancestors, but it is certain that most of them were brought to America from Africa in chains, in the holds of slave ships. (The hold is the lower part of a ship where the cargo is stored.) Only Tubman's maternal grandmother, Modesty, is known by name. According to Franklin Sanborn, an early Tubman biographer, Tubman was "a granddaughter of a slave born in Africa and has not a drop of white blood in her veins." The latter part of that statement may not have been true, but many biographers believe that Tubman's grandmother Modesty was Ashanti, a member of an ethnic group from what today is Ghana, in West Africa. During the eighteenth century, more than one million slaves were bought by British, Danish, and Dutch slave traders and shipped to the Americas from the Ashanti Empire on West Africa's Gold Coast, a rich trading region. Many Ashanti slaves were sold to buyers in Maryland.

Tubman's mother, Harriet Green, was known as Rittia or Rit. Rittia was born a slave, but she may have had a white father. This was not uncommon in slaveholding households. Such relationships between slaves and their white owners were sometimes forced and were never equal because of the imbalance of power. Slaves, like other possessions such as houses and furniture, were passed down through families. Rittia, and probably Rittia's mother and grandmother, was owned by a woman named Mary Pattison Brodess. After the death of Brodess's first husband, she married again. Her new husband was Anthony Thompson, the wealthy owner of a timber plantation in Dorchester County, Maryland. When she moved to the Thompson house, Brodess brought her slaves with her. Rittia worked in the house as a cook.

It was on the Thompson plantation that Rittia probably met Benjamin Ross, one of Thompson's slaves. Ross was a supervisor in Thompson's timber business. When the timber on Thompson's plantation was cut, it was hauled to Baltimore. There, it was put on ships and sold up and down the East Coast of the United States. Not much is known about Ben Ross's parents or grandparents. Together, Rittia and Ben Ross had nine children. Their names were Linah, Mariah Ritty, Soph, Rachel, Robert, Ben, Henry, Moses, and, of course, Araminta. After Mary Pattison Brodess Thompson died, her slaves, including Rittia and her children, were inherited by her son, Edward Brodess.

The fact that Araminta's parents had different owners was significant. A few years after Araminta's birth, the family was torn apart. When Edward Brodess married, in 1824, he moved with his wife to a house in Bucktown, about 10 miles from the Thompson plantation. Brodess took Rittia and her children with him, but Ben Ross probably was left behind to continue his work in the timber business. According to researchers, Brodess also made some money by selling off some of Rittia's children. In 1855, as an adult, Tubman recalled the painful loss of two sisters. "I had two sisters carried away in a chain-gang— one of them left two children. We were always uneasy." Four of Tubman's eight siblings may have been sold before Tubman escaped to freedom. Three of her sisters—Linah, Mariah Ritty, and Soph—disappeared and were lost to the family, according to some sources.

A NEGLECTED WEED

Today, Araminta's birthplace on Thompson's plantation has disappeared, and archaeologists have not found remnants there of the family's life. It is not hard, however, to imagine the countryside that Tubman must have seen every day as a young girl. The low-lying rural landscape near the Chesapeake Bay was lush and green, with mild winters and warm, muggy summers. Fields of oats, potatoes, corn, and hay, peach orchards, and grist mills dotted the fertile acreage, along with forests of oak, hickory, pine, and walnut trees, all of which were harvested for building and the shipping industry. Winding through the area were the slow-moving rivers and estuaries that flowed into the bay, where hauls of oysters, shad, and herring brought in profits for fishermen.

Near where Tubman grew up, the small town of Bucktown boasted a few stores, a blacksmith shop, and several shipyards on the Transquaking River. Today, the Blackwater National Wildlife Refuge—a protected area of wetlands, fields, and forests where birdwatchers aim their binoculars at eagles and osprey—is nearby. Because young Araminta spent so much of her childhood outdoors, often working in the fields, she was well aware of the natural world around her. Her familiarity with the swamps and fields helped her when she had to steal away in the dead of night.

Work was the activity that shaped Araminta's early years. The children of slaves were expected to benefit their owners as quickly as possible. They did not have a childhood. Often, older children had to care for their younger siblings while their mothers worked six days a week. As Araminta's mother spent long hours cooking in the main house, Araminta watched the younger children. Isolated on plantations, without schooling or freedom, slave children had little hope for the future. Araminta never was taught to read and write. In 1855, after her escape to freedom in Canada, Tubman said, "I grew up like a neglected weed ignorant of liberty, having no experience of it. Then I was not happy or contented; every time I saw a white man I was afraid of being carried away." Her fears were well-founded. All too soon, Araminta was carried away from her family.

To supplement his income, Edward Brodess rented his slaves, including Araminta, to other families in the area. Slave owners often rented their slaves to gain extra cash. As a grown woman, Tubman told her biographer Ednah Cheney that Edward Brodess was "never unnecessarily cruel," but he often sent his slaves to others who were. Some of them, she said, "proved to be tyrannical and brutal to the utmost limit of their power." According to Tubman, she was just five years old when a white woman known as Miss Susan came by to ask Brodess for a slave girl to take care of her baby. Brodess sent her Araminta. In later life, Tubman told the story to a sympathetic white teacher named Sarah Bradford. Bradford interviewed Tubman and wrote two biographies. The first, *Scenes in the Life of Harriet Tubman*, was published in 1869. The second, a revised version called *The Moses of Her People*, was published in 1886. As Tubman recalled, she was miserable in her new home. She was terribly homesick and unused to having to eat with white people.

Araminta cried herself to sleep on the hard floor. Too young to do the housework well enough to please her new mistress, she was scolded and punished often. Miss Susan's sister, a woman named Miss Emily, tried to come to Araminta's aid and show her how to do her chores, but to little avail. Barely older than her young charge, Araminta had to sit on the floor to hold the baby. She was told to stay up all night and rock the baby's cradle so that the baby did not wake. If the baby cried, Araminta was whipped. One day, Tubman told Bradford, she was whipped five times before breakfast. "Her neck bore the scar from this incident for the rest of her life," writes biographer Catherine Clinton, in *Harriet Tubman: The Road to Freedom*. When Araminta finally was sent home, she was hungry and weak.

"VITTLES AND CLOTHES"

Araminta's mother cared for her until she was better, but she couldn't stop Brodess from sending her young daughter out to work, again and again. Tubman later remembered that she rarely lived at home during her childhood. She called it being "put out again for vittles and clothes." Yet, even as a young girl sent to work in strangers' houses, Araminta displayed the independent streak that carried her through her difficult life.

When she was about seven, the master and mistress of the house where Araminta was working had a quarrel. Araminta saw that they were not watching her, and she sneaked a lump of sugar from the table. "Now, you know, I never had anything good, no sweet, no sugar, and that sugar, right by me, did look so nice . . . So I just put my fingers in the sugar bowl to take one lump and maybe she heard me for she turned and saw me." To escape her punishment—a rawhide whip—Araminta ran out the door. Too scared to return, she wandered around until she found herself inside a pigpen. There she stayed for several days, miserably living with the pigs, until she finally got up the courage to return to the house and face her punishment.

During the times she was sent out to work, Araminta was forced to do many jobs. Most of them were unfit for anyone, much less a child. At one time, Araminta was hired out to work for a hunter and trapper. She was made to wade into a pond to remove dead muskrats from a trap, even though she was ill, possibly with the measles. At another time, she worked for a weaver, breaking flax. As she grew older, she was hired out to a farmer to work in the fields. The treatment she received was often as bad as the work she was given to do. One mistress whipped her so often that Araminta wore many layers of clothing to shield herself from the pain. As an adult, Tubman described herself as a weak and sickly child. This was not surprising, given what she had to endure.

THE BUSINESS OF SLAVERY

While Araminta was growing up, slavery was an established system of labor in Maryland and in many other states. According to Kate Clifford Larson, in *Bound for the Promised Land*, her biography of Harriet Tubman, about 18,000 African slaves landed at the ports of Maryland during the mid-eighteenth century. It wasn't until 1864—during the Civil War and after Tubman had fled from Maryland—that the state abolished slavery.

The European slave trade began in earnest in the 1430s, when Portuguese merchants sailed down the African coast in search of gold. Instead of precious metal, the merchants found a new profit-making commodity: human slaves. Slavery already was part of the African social structure, but the selling of slaves for export brought the practice to a new level. The Portuguese began buying African slaves and selling them to purchasers in Europe and in the Muslim world. Other Europeans, including the Dutch and, later, the British, followed suit.

When Europeans established colonies in the Americas, slavery came with them. The settlers wanted cheap labor to build their new lives and businesses. The slave trade expanded from the Old World to the New, across the Atlantic Ocean. It came first to the islands of the Caribbean, where plantation owners used African laborers in the backbreaking work of sugarcane planting and harvesting.

The transatlantic slave trade reached the shores of North America in 1619, when 20 Africans were sold off a ship in Jamestown, Virginia. Before that date, the earliest colonists had used indentured servants as help on farms and in households. Indentured servants were poor Europeans who received free passage across the Atlantic in return for several years of unpaid labor. At the end of the period of indenture, these servants were given their freedom. American Indians also were used as indentured servants, and some American Indians were kept as slaves.

Maryland was one of the first states to legalize slavery, in 1664. By 1690, because of the establishment of tobacco plantations and a growing demand for field workers, the number of African slaves brought to Maryland began to increase. Here, and throughout the other North American colonies, slaves became an important part of the labor force. During the next century, slaves worked for tobacco farmers in Maryland, for brickmakers in Philadelphia, and for cotton planters in the Carolinas. Some of the Founding Fathers of the United States, including George Washington and Thomas Jefferson, were slave owners.

In 2007, Jamestown, Virginia, celebrated its 400th year of existence. Jamestown was the first permanent English settlement
in what is now the United States, but was also the first to intro-
duce slavery to America. Dutch traders brought 20 slaves from
Angola, in southwest Africa, to work the tobacco plantations.
The painting above depicts the arrival of the first slaves on the
Dutch slave ship *Man-of-War* in 1619.

THE LIFE OF AN AMERICAN SLAVE

"A slave may be bought and sold in the market like an ox. He is to be sold off to a distant land from his family. He is bound in chains hand and foot; and his sufferings are aggravated a hundred fold, by the terrible thought, that he is not allowed to struggle against misfortune, corporeal punishment, insults and outrages committed upon himself and family; and he is not allowed to help himself, to resist or escape the blow, which he sees impending over him."

Those are the words of Henry Bibb, who was born a slave in Kentucky in about 1813. He tried many times to flee from his owners, but he always was caught and returned. During his life as a slave, Bibb was traded to several different owners. His last owner was a Cherokee Indian in Kansas or Oklahoma. Bibb finally escaped through Missouri and Ohio and settled in Detroit. Bibb learned to read and write as an adult and began to lecture against slavery with other abolitionists—men and women who spoke out and fought to abolish slavery. Bibb's autobiography, *Narrative of the Life and Adventures of Henry Bibb, An American Slave, Written by Himself*, was published in New York in 1849. Bibb's heartbreaking account added a new voice to the growing cry to end slavery. Bibb later moved to Canada, where he opened a school and started Canada's first black newspaper, *Voice of the Fugitive*. Here is another excerpt from his book:

I have often worked without half enough to eat, both late and early, by day and by night. I have often laid my wearied limbs down at night to rest upon a dirt floor, or a bench, without any covering at all, because I had no where else to rest my wearied body, after having worked hard all the day. I have also been compelled in early life, to go at the bidding of a tyrant, through all kinds of weather, hot or cold, wet or dry, and without shoes frequently, until the month of December, with my bare feet on the cold frosty ground, cracked open and bleeding as I walked.

THE COTTON GIN INCREASES DEMAND FOR SLAVES

With more new European immigrants able to provide cheap labor, the need for slaves lessened by the end of the 1700s. The slave trade to the United States was banned in 1808, although smuggling continued. In 1793, however, with Eli Whitney's invention of the cotton gin, slavery experienced a revival. The cotton gin made it easier to process cotton, and the cotton industry expanded rapidly. The economies of many Southern states soon grew dependent on cotton. Farmers needed slaves to work their expanding cotton fields. In the years leading up to the outbreak of the Civil War in 1861, there were 4 million slaves in the United States.

As time went on, after the ban on the African slave trade, most slaves no longer were African born. Instead, on the rice plantations of South Carolina and in the sweet potato fields of Alabama, great numbers of slaves were American born. Some of these enslaved Americans were born on the plantations where they worked; others were bought or traded from owners of other plantations. Slave owners encouraged their slaves to have many children because good money was to be made by trading and renting slaves who were not needed at home. In this way, the system of slavery strengthened its hold on the American South. Masters had few rules to follow when it came to handling their slaves. Some slaves were promised their freedom after a certain number of years. In fact, Harriet Tubman's father, Benjamin Ross, was freed by his owner.

In 1829, the chief justice of North Carolina, Thomas Ruffin, reflected the attitude of his time when he wrote, in the case of *State v. Mann*, "The power of the master must be absolute, to render the submission of the slave perfect."

Before the invention of the cotton gin, seeds had to be removed from cotton fibers by hand, which took a long time and required large amounts of effort. Although the gin damages the fiber, it allowed the seeds to be removed mechanically and rapidly. This upsurge in production led to the dramatic growth of the cotton industry, leading to an increase of slave labor in the United States.

Before the nineteenth century, very few people in America raised their voices to criticize the practice of slavery. The organized drive to end slavery—the abolitionist movement—did not make an impact until the 1830s. During Araminta's childhood, slavery was deeply entrenched in the United States. Araminta, however, was not willing to submit, silently and forever, to a life of slavery.

"Liberty, or Death"

When she was in her teens, Araminta was rented out by her owner to work in the fields at a neighboring farm during the harvest. One day, a young slave ran off without permission. The overseer chased him to a local store at a crossroads in Buckstown. Araminta may have followed the runaway, or she might have been at the store on an errand. According to some versions of the story, she was asked to help restrain the boy but did not. When he tried to flee, Araminta blocked the door so that the overseer could not pursue him. In other versions, Araminta, wrapped in a shawl, was a bystander.

However the incident may have happened, the result was the same. The overseer picked up an iron weight and threw it toward the boy. The weight hit Araminta's head, fracturing her skull. "That weight struck me in the head and broke my skull and cut a piece of that shawl clean off and drove it into my head. They carried me to the house all bleeding and fainting," Tubman told biographer Emma Telford in 1905. Because she did not have a bed at the house, those who carried her there placed her on the seat of the weaving loom. She stayed there for two days, until those in charge made her go to work again. "I worked with the blood and sweat rolling downs my face till I couldn't see," she later said.

Araminta nearly died from the injury. For months, she slowly recovered, but her health was permanently damaged. For the rest of her life, she suffered from severe headaches and seizures. She sometimes lost consciousness in the middle of a conversation and seemed to go to sleep. She then started talking again a few minutes later, as if nothing had happened. After her terrible injury, young Araminta grew more religious. She prayed frequently, often out loud. Tubman told people that during her blackouts, she had visions from God.

A STRONG RELIGIOUS FAITH

Religion was an important part of the lives of African-American slaves. Their faith helped them to survive the humiliations of their daily lives. It also inspired them and gave them hope for a brighter future of freedom. Some slaves practiced Islam. The faith of Islam was followed by many people in West Africa, the region from which the slave traders had taken their ancestors. As time went on, many slaves converted to Christianity, the faith of their owners' families. Sometimes, however, Christian preachers and ministers who were part of the slave-owning society justified slavery in their sermons. Abolitionists criticized this use of religion to support slavery.

Frederick Douglass, a runaway slave who became a leading abolitionist, was especially incensed at this misuse of religion. In a speech delivered in London, England, in 1846, Douglass said: "Why, we have slavery made part of the religion of the land. Yes,

Slaves were forbidden from practicing African religious practices, and were inundated by their masters' preachers with messages about obedience and servitude. In response, slaves held secret religious meetings in the night to sing and pray about their sufferings and to practice the way they wanted. Despite the threat of flogging, slaves continued to hold their own religious gatherings.

the pulpit there stands up as the great defender of this cursed *institution*, as it is called. Ministers of religion come forward and torture the hallowed pages of inspired wisdom to sanction the bloody deed. They stand forth as the foremost, the strongest defenders of this 'institution.'"

Slave communities often met to pray in secret, defying laws against groups of slaves gathering or holding meetings. In these meetings, the slaves spoke of the New Testament's promises of the day of reckoning and justice, and of a better life after death. African-American slaves felt a bond with the Old Testament

SLAVE SPIRITUALS

Even when they were locked in chains in the holds of slave ships crossing the Atlantic, captive Africans bound for the tobacco fields of Maryland and the rice plantations of South Carolina turned to song to express their desire for freedom. Some historians have said that desperate slaves who jumped overboard to avoid their fate fell into the water singing. Through song, slaves tried to turn their suffering into joy, at least temporarily, and pulled together as a community.

The spirituals—religious songs—that slaves sang on the plantations of the American South had roots in African music. These songs were filled not only with religious faith, but also with a sense of history. Spirituals expressed a full range of emotions, from hope to despair. Many spirituals were based on the stories of Biblical figures such as Moses and Joshua, heroes who led the Hebrew slaves from Egyptian bondage to freedom. In the spiritual "Go Down Moses," the words tell of the slaves' desire for freedom: "Go down, Moses/Way down in Egypt land./Tell old Pharaoh/To let my people go." Spirituals often gave voice to the theme of slaves as the chosen people—chosen, like the Israelites, despite their lowly position in the slave-owning society. In these songs, the slaves are chosen by God not only to endure great suffering, but also to be rewarded in the end.

Some spirituals were protest songs. Their words expressed righteous defiance against the bonds of slavery and the troubles endured in daily life. For the slaves who embarked on the Underground Railroad, the spirituals they sang and heard contained coded messages that helped them to plot their escapes or convey messages to others. Harriet

(continues)

(continued)

Tubman used her strong singing voice to communicate with other fugitives and other conductors on the Underground Railroad through the lyrics in spirituals. According to Tubman biographer Kate Clifford Larson, in *Bound for the Promised Land*, "If danger lurked nearby, Tubman would sing an appropriate spiritual to warn her party of an impending threat to their safety." The famous spiritual "Steal Away," for example, might signal that an escaping slave should prepare to leave; that help was near:

> "Steal away, steal away,
> Steal away to Jesus,
> Steal away, steal away home,
> I ain't got long to stay here."

story of Exodus, in which Moses leads the Israelites out of slavery in Egypt, across the Red Sea to God's mountain. Later, Moses' assistant Joshua leads the Israelites to the River Jordan. The waters dry up, and they cross the dry riverbed to the land of Canaan, where they are free.

Slaves spoke of the North as "Canaan" and described the obstacles to freedom as the River Jordan. Members of Araminta's family sometimes attended church with their owners. They also may have met with other enslaved families at makeshift churches in the woods. Wherever Araminta may have learned her religion, her faith was deep, unwavering, and very personal. "Hers was not the religion of a morning and evening prayer at stated times, but when she felt a need, she simply told God of it, and trusted Him to set the matter right," wrote Sarah

Bradford. After Araminta's injury, she also began to have dreams and visions. Those visions, along with her religious faith, led her through great difficulties and pointed the way when there seemed to be no light in sight.

MARRIAGE

Although she never fully recovered, with time and her mother's care, Araminta slowly healed from her injury. Despite her weakness, Araminta's owners still tried to make money from her by renting her out to work. In about 1835, Araminta was hired out to John T. Stewart, whose father, Joseph, was one of the wealthiest slaveholders in the county. The Stewart family ran a large farm and had many businesses, including lumbering, a windmill, and shipbuilding. Araminta's father and brothers also sometimes worked for the Stewarts.

Araminta did many jobs during the five or six years she worked for the Stewarts and other local families. The days were always long, and she worked from dawn to dusk. She may have worked in the house, beating the feather beds and cleaning. Mostly, however, she worked outside, possibly lifting barrels for the Stewarts' store, pulling boats down the canals, and packing grain for the windmill, according to Kate Clifford Larson. Eventually, Araminta became a field worker. She drove oxen, cut wood, and plowed the earth for planting.

Araminta grew to be only about five feet tall, but her short stature did not prevent her from performing labor usually done by men. Araminta worked so hard that she was able to earn a little money for herself. After she paid her owner the wage he demanded, she could keep the extra money. In time, she saved enough to buy a pair of steers worth $40 and was able to hire herself and her pair out to earn more money. Perhaps one day, she thought, she could earn her way to freedom.

Around 1844, when Araminta was in her twenties, she married a free black man named John Tubman, and she took his last name. Slaves could not be legally married, nor were their marriages protected from interference by their owners. Often, a marriage was just a matter of two slaves getting permission to move in with each other. There was no ceremony or legal document. After a slave couple married, if they lived on different plantations, they had to get permission from their owners to visit each other. Even worse, slave couples could be separated or sold at the will of their owners.

Because of their work, Araminta and her new husband may not have lived together. Little is known about John Tubman, such as whether he was born a slave. Although slaves were encouraged to have children to provide more workers for their owners, historians have found no sign that Harriet Tubman ever had children, either with John or with her second husband, whom she married after she escaped from slavery. Some researchers have wondered whether a foster daughter whom Tubman rescued from Maryland and took to her home in upstate New York in the 1850s was really her daughter, but no proof has been uncovered.

FREEDOM, DELAYED

For many years, Araminta suspected that her mother should have been freed years earlier. Slave owners often promised in writing to free their slaves at a certain age. They did not want to care for elderly men and women who were too old to work. After the transatlantic slave trade ended in 1808, and no more African slaves were shipped into the country, even older slaves became more valuable, however. Giving slaves their freedom was like giving away money. Because of this, many slave owners ignored agreements to set their older slaves free.

Araminta was determined to learn the truth about her mother's right to freedom. Around 1845, she hired a lawyer and paid him $5 to look up the will of her mother's first master. The lawyer found a will from 1791 stating that Rittia and her future children were given to the master's granddaughter, Mary Pattison, to serve until Rittia turned 45. Rittia's children also would serve only until age 45. Araminta was upset to learn that her mother should have been freed about 10 years earlier. "It was the discovery of this betrayal that fueled her resolve to liberate herself," wrote biographer Catherine Clinton.

Araminta's father had a different owner, and Ben Ross was more fortunate. Anthony Thompson had promised Ross his freedom at age 45. Thompson died, but his son, Dr. Anthony C. Thompson, honored his father's promise. In 1840, Ross gained his freedom. He stayed with Thompson as a free laborer in his timber business. When Dr. Thompson bought a new property known as Poplar Neck, full of hickory and oak trees, Ross went there to oversee the timber operation. The new property was located farther inland, in Caroline County, Maryland. Ross probably took his wife along, and his sons worked there, too. Araminta also worked for the Thompson family, from 1847 to 1849.

ESCAPE

Tubman's father was free, and so was her husband. Tubman dreamed of crossing the River Jordan to the land of Canaan. Desperately unhappy, she began to pray that her master, Edward Brodess, would become more Christian and moral. She even wished for his death. When that death came unexpectedly early, Tubman felt a little guilty. As she told Sarah Bradford: "Then I changed my prayer, and I said, 'Lord, if you ain't never going to change that man's heart, kill him, Lord, and take him out of the way, so he won't do no more mischief.' Next thing I heard old master was dead; and he died just as he had lived, a wicked, bad man. Oh, then it appeared like I would give the world full of silver and gold, if I had it, to bring that poor soul back, I would give myself; I would give everything! But he was gone, I couldn't pray for him no more."

Edward Brodess died unexpectedly in 1849, at the age of 47. His will left Rittia and her children to his wife, Eliza Ann, to help raise their children. Brodess's death raised new fears for

Tubman. The death of a slave owner sometimes led to the sale of the slaves to pay debts. Tubman already had seen several of her siblings sold away. At least two sisters, Linah and Soph, were sold to slaveholders in other states, never to be seen again. The fear of being sold gave Tubman nightmares. She told Sarah Bradford that "she never closed her eyes that she did not imagine she saw the horsemen coming, and heard the screams of women and children, as they were being dragged away to a far worse slavery than that they were enduring there."

Then Tubman heard that two of her brothers were to be sold to help pay the Brodess family's debts. Tubman worried that she, too, might be "sold far South," to a worse slave owner and even harsher conditions. It was time for her to go. Slaves planning to escape had to keep their plans quiet. Rather than telling family and friends directly, they might sing a song with a secret message encoded in the lyrics. In the night, among the slave cabins, according to some accounts, Araminta did just that. "When that old chariot comes, I'm going to leave you, I'm bound for the promised land, Friends, I'm going to leave you," she sang.

MINTY IS GONE

On about September 17, 1849, Araminta and her brothers Ben and Henry sneaked away from the Thompson plantation at Poplar Neck. A local newspaper, the *Cambridge Democrat*, printed a notice about three runaway slaves. The notice announced rewards for the return of the three, "MINTY, aged about 27 years, . . . of a chestnut color, fine looking, and bout [sic] 5 feet high," and her two brothers. The reward was $50 if the runaways were found in Maryland or $100 if they were found out of state. The notice was signed by Eliza Brodess. After two or three weeks, the trio apparently returned, unable to complete their journey to freedom. As Bradford wrote in her biography of Tubman, "The brothers started with her, but the way was strange, the north was far away, and all unknown, the

QUILT CODES: TRUTH OR MYTH?

Separating truth from myth is a challenge for anyone researching the Underground Railroad. Much of what happened during the thousands of escapes to freedom was not documented. In the absence of verifiable facts, myths based on what little is known have emerged. In recent years, a controversy has arisen over quilt codes. According to those who have researched and written about quilt codes, the geometric patterns in slave-made quilts were used to send messages along the Underground Railroad.

In 1993, Deborah Hopkinson wrote a children's picture book, *Sweet Clara and the Freedom Quilt*, about a slave who escaped by using a quilt that looked like a map. In 1999, Jacqueline Tobin and Raymond G. Dobard, Ph.D, wrote *Hidden in Plain View: A Secret Story of Quilts and the Underground Railroad*, a nonfiction book about quilt codes. Tobin had met a woman in South Carolina who said that her family had handed down stories about sewing patterns into quilts to serve as directions for slaves trying to escape.

More books and museum exhibits have followed. Some historians say, however, that without concrete evidence, it is questionable whether quilt codes really existed. Critics also say that focusing on quilt codes takes away from the study of the real suffering of slaves and of the struggles they endured to escape to freedom. In 2007, New York City planned to erect a statue of abolitionist and former slave Frederick Douglass in a plaza of quilt patterns in Central Park. Several historians protested against the use of quilts in the exhibit.

(continues)

(continued)

"The Underground Railroad is one of the deepest American historical myths," said historian David Blight in a 2007 interview on the radio program "All Things Considered." In Blight's words: "It is a story of escape; it is a story from slavery to freedom. The problem has been: How do we carve through the enormous folklore and mythology of this story to get to the real stories of real fugitive slaves?"

Other historians point out that the courageous and secret efforts that slaves made to send messages under the noses of their white owners, whether in the lyrics of spirituals or sewn into quilts, will never be fully known. Quilting was part of the slave culture, and many women sewed family quilts. Tubman was skilled at quilting, and she is said to have given a quilt to a white woman in exchange for help in Tubman's escape to freedom in Philadelphia.

masters would pursue and recapture them, and their fate would be worse than before."

Soon after, Tubman set off alone. Ninety miles stretched between her home in Maryland and the free state of Pennsylvania. She would have to cross through Delaware, a state with few slaves but with strict laws that restricted free blacks. The distance was far and the obstacles many for someone moving on foot. Runaways typically could travel about 10 miles per day, and they usually traveled at night. Tubman probably had never left her home county or been on her own before. She had no money, and she faced grave danger. Slaves were not allowed to roam freely off their plantations. If caught, they were arrested, beaten, and returned to their owners.

Alone and at risk of capture, Tubman had to find her way through unfamiliar territory with only the North Star to guide her. That bright star is located at the very end of the handle of the constellation known as the Little Dipper. The North Star served as both a symbol and a navigational guide for escaping slaves because it points the way due north. Tubman's determination was stronger than any obstacles. As she later told Sarah Bradford, "I had reasoned this out in my mind; there was one of two things I had a right to, liberty, or death; if I could not have one, I would have the other; for no man should take me alive; I should fight for my liberty as long as my strength lasted, and when the time came for me to go, the Lord would let them take me." Not knowing what lay ahead, Tubman broke the bonds of slavery and set forth on a new path to freedom.

UNDERGROUND RAILROAD

At some point, Tubman changed her name from Araminta to Harriet, which was her mother's name. Some biographers think that she made the change when she got married. Others say that she did it when she escaped to freedom. Many runaway slaves took new names to protect themselves against being recognized by slave catchers and sent back to the plantations from which they had fled.

Little is known about Tubman's journey to freedom. She may not have been completely on her own. She later said that a white woman scribbled two names and an address on a piece of paper, even though Tubman could not read. In return, Tubman gave the woman a quilt that she had made. The white woman would have been part of a network of people, both black and white, who helped slaves to escape to the North and to Canada by providing directions, money, food, a secure room in an attic or closet, and moral support. This network was begun by a few Quakers—members of the Religious Society of Friends—in Philadelphia. Eventually, the loosely organized system expanded to hundreds of people in many states and in Canada.

The Quaker abolitionist Isaac T. Hopper is one of the "fathers" of the Underground Railroad. He helped fugitive slaves as early as 1790 in Philadelphia. Many others also risked their personal safety to aid the fugitive slaves, breaking the law in the process. These helpers included free and enslaved blacks who lived in slave states, wealthy citizens in New York City and Philadelphia, and humble farmers in rural Delaware. In his book *Bound for Canaan*, Underground Railroad researcher Fergus M. Bordewich calls it "the nation's first great movement of civil disobedience since the American Revolution." For the first time, Bordewich suggests, people were taking responsibility for other people's human rights.

The term *Underground Railroad* emerged in the 1830s to describe the secret network. The era of steam locomotives began during the same decade. People saw railroad tracks being laid across the country and passenger trains starting to travel through Baltimore and New York City. Abolitionists recognized a similarity between their effort to move slaves to freedom and the trains that carried passengers from one city to another. To emphasize this resemblance, workers on the Underground Railroad used the same terms as workers on the railroad. The paths the fugitives took were called "tracks." The safe houses were "stations" or "depots." The fugitive slaves were "passengers" or "parcels." The people who protected and led the runaway slaves were "conductors," and the people who offered their homes as safe havens were "stationmasters."

Even though it was compared to a real railroad, the Underground Railroad was made up of people, not locomotives, passenger cars, and tracks. Nor was the system truly underground. No tunnels or below-ground passageways have been found. Sometimes the fugitives traveled on foot through forests. Sometimes they rowed or sailed boats on rivers or took steamboats up the coast. Sometimes they went on roads via horse and buggy. Sometimes they even traveled by train. Along the way were safe houses where the travelers found

Even at the height of the Underground Railroad, only a small amount of slaves were able to escape. Due to the danger and difficulty of the journey, most escapees were men. The primary means of transportation for fugitives was on foot or by wagon and indirect routes were used to throw off pursuers. In this painting, three men help an escaped slave hide from slave catchers who are in pursuit.

shelter, food, and safety. The most important links, however, were the people.

In the past, storytellers and historians focused on the white "conductors" and other helpers who bravely disobeyed the law to hide the fugitives. Recently, historians have emphasized that black men and women, both free and enslaved, were just as important to the Underground Railroad as whites. The National Park Service has created a network of sites important to the Underground Railroad, which it describes as "the effort of enslaved African Americans to gain freedom by escaping bondage." Tubman became the best-known conductor of all.

By 1849, the Underground Railroad network was moving hundreds of slaves to freedom each year, mostly from the border states nearest to the free North. There were several routes, including two main routes that ran east of the Appalachian Mountains. Slaves in the Deep South also fled from their owners, but those fugitives did not often make it all the way to the North. In the three decades before the Civil War, the Underground Railroad reached its peak. In those years, it guided perhaps 100,000 slaves in all; no one knows the exact numbers. For every fugitive, the journey was unique.

In her later years, Tubman told people that she still dreamed about her journey to freedom. She dreamed that she was "flying over fields and towns, and rivers and mountains, looking down upon them 'like a bird' and reaching at last a great fence, or sometimes a river, over which she would try to fly." When Tubman finally crossed the Mason-Dixon Line that marked the boundary between the Southern states and the free state of Pennsylvania, she stepped into a new world. What lay ahead, she had no idea. She had never walked a city street alone or spoken to white people who were not her owners or bosses. She must not have had the vaguest idea of how she would survive. Her deep sense of purpose and her faith showed her the way.

"The Midnight Sky and Silent Stars"

In 1849, Tubman arrived in Philadelphia. It was a bustling and industrious city with a history of antislavery activity. Founded by the English Quaker leader William Penn in 1682, Philadelphia was built on a philosophy of religious tolerance and freedom of conscience. Many of the Quakers who emigrated from England to Philadelphia and the rest of the colony of Pennsylvania were abolitionists. Even so, in 1684, the ship *Isabella* docked in Philadelphia to unload and sell 150 African slaves. Many more slave ships delivered human cargo from Africa to Philadelphia in the decades that followed. In Philadelphia, the slaves worked as carpenters, domestic servants, sailmakers, bakers, and in other trades. Antislavery sentiment was growing, however. The state of Pennsylvania passed a law

Quaker William Penn founded the city of Philadelphia in Pennsylvania (pictured above in 1844). Colonial Pennsylvania began as a slave-owning society and Penn was the owner of 12 slaves, but the Northern economy and politics became factors in slavery's demise. Some Quakers had been debating the morality of owning slaves for dozens of years, and in 1779 Pennsylvania passed the first abolition law in America (although the law did not emancipate a single slave until 1847).

in 1779 that called for the gradual abolition of slavery. It took effect in 1780.

In the 1790s, protestors tried to block the slave ships from docking in Philadelphia. The earliest antislavery society in Great Britain's North American colonies was founded in this city, and other local organizations helped to fight against fugitive slave laws. By 1840, there were fewer than 100 slaves in Pennsylvania. Slavery was abolished in the state in 1847. By the time Tubman arrived there, Philadelphia was a relatively

SLAVERY AND THE CONSTITUTION

Philadelphia was the new nation's capital in 1787, when 55 lawmakers met there to hammer out the United States Constitution. Many of those men were either present or former slave owners. The delegates gathered in the red-brick Pennsylvania State House on Chestnut Street—the building known today as Independence Hall—to write a document that promised to "secure the blessings of liberty." The final document did not offer liberty to everyone, however. It excluded African-American slaves.

The Constitution embodied a compromise between Southerners who wanted to keep importing slaves and to count slaves in their state populations and Northerners who were against slavery but wanted a signed Constitution. Thus, the Constitution permitted the slave trade to continue for two more decades and allowed the capture of fugitive slaves. According to Section 2, Article 4, of the Constitution:

> No person held to service or labour in one state, under the laws thereof, escaping into another, shall, in consequence of any law or regulation therein, be discharged from such service or labour, but shall be delivered up on claim of the party to whom such service or labour may be due.

The word *slavery* was not used, but it was understood. For purposes of tallying population, the Constitution allowed states to count each slave as "three fifths of a person."

The white abolitionist William Lloyd Garrison stated that the founding of the nation was "a covenant with death" and an "agreement with hell." In 1987, on the 200th anniversary

(continues)

(continued)

of the Constitution, former United States Supreme Court justice Thurgood Marshall—the high court's first African-American justice—said that he did not "find the wisdom, foresight, and sense of justice exhibited by the Framers particularly profound. The government they devised was defective from the start."

safe destination for runaway slaves. Many white and black abolitionists in the city offered shelter and assistance to fugitive slaves on their way north to safety and freedom.

In Philadelphia, as a small woman in her late twenties, Harriet Tubman probably blended in and did not attract attention because of her race as she might have done in other cities. By 1860, Philadelphia was home to about 22,000 African Americans. The city had the largest black population of any city in the North. On Sundays, the city's 16 black churches were filled with worshippers. There were schools for black children, and social organizations such as temperance societies (groups that spoke out against the use of alcoholic beverages) and literary groups helped to bring the community together.

In some ways, however, the city also was divided. Blacks were crowded into poorer neighborhoods and had trouble finding jobs. Starting in the 1840s, immigrants poured into Pennsylvania from Germany and Ireland, and the divide between the rich and the poor grew. The Quaker spirit of tolerance was not shared by everyone in Philadelphia. Riots broke out between blacks and whites, and the homes of black citizens were burned. The meetinghouses where abolitionists gathered were sometimes torched, as well.

FIRST TASTE OF FREEDOM

It was in this city of contrasts that Tubman experienced her first year of freedom. She found employment as a cook and household worker, possibly in hotels. During the summer, she worked at Cape May, a summer resort town on the New Jersey shore that was a short distance away. With her wages, Tubman was able not only to support herself but also to save some money. She took in a nephew and paid for his schooling. She also got to know abolitionists and antislavery activists and learned about politics and about events that she could not have known as a field worker in Maryland.

Tubman became friends with William Still, a free black who worked at the American Anti-Slavery Society's office in Philadelphia and was a leader on the Underground Railroad. Abolitionists in Philadelphia organized a Vigilance Committee, led by Still, to help fugitive slaves on their way to New York and Canada. The runaway slaves stopped at Still's office, where he often slipped them money for their journey. In his famous book, *The Underground Rail Road Records*, Still told the stories of the ex-slaves whom he had helped on their way. He described Tubman like this:

> a woman of no pretensions, indeed, a more ordinary specimen of humanity could hardly be found among the most unfortunate-looking farm hands of the South. Yet, in point of courage, shrewdness and disinterested exertions to rescue her fellow-men . . . she was without her equal.

Tubman also was acquainted with James and Lucretia Mott, leaders in the antislavery and women's rights movements, and many others. Lucretia Mott would remain her friend for many years.

Still, it was hard for Tubman to enjoy her freedom while her relatives, slave and free, remained in a slave state. She had always been close to the members of her large family, and she

Abolitionist William Still (1821–1902) is often called the "Father of the Underground Railroad" for helping as many as 60 slaves a month to escape. He kept careful records of each person, and during one interview he discovered that the fugitive was his brother Peter. Later, Still published the book *The Underground Rail Road Records*, one of the few chronicles that provided real accounts of the methods and biographies of escaped slaves.

missed them deeply. She must have been very lonely in the unfamiliar city where no one knew her well. "I was a stranger in a strange land. My father, my mother, my brothers, and sisters, and friends were [in Maryland]. But I was free, and they should be free," she later told Sarah Bradford. Tubman wanted her relatives to join her, but she knew how difficult it was to escape on one's own. A little over a year after she arrived in Philadelphia, she returned to Maryland to make her first rescue, but a new federal law made her journey more perilous than ever.

THE FUGITIVE SLAVE ACT OF 1850

By the 1840s, the Southern states were trying to save the institution of slavery. The cotton fields of Georgia and the tobacco plantations of Virginia required intense labor. Farmers relied on their unpaid workers to plant and harvest the crops. The slaveholders feared that their way of life was endangered, however. Periodic slave uprisings made white people more anxious and determined to control their slaves. In 1832, a slave in Southampton County, Virginia, led a daring slave uprising with tragic results. Nat Turner and his followers went from house to house, freeing slaves and killing 57 white men, women, and children. Turner and about 55 other slaves were caught and executed by the state of Virginia, and white mobs went after other blacks, killing about 200 people. At the same time, the Underground Railroad was growing, and the abolitionist movement was gaining followers. The nation's courts were debating how far to go to protect slavery. In 1842, in a case titled *Prigg v. Pennsylvania*, the U.S. Supreme Court decided that free states did not have to return runaway slaves.

Slave owners worried about losing their valuable human property. They wanted stronger laws to protect their rights. The state of Maryland passed new laws that restricted the rights of free blacks and forbade slave owners from freeing their slaves unless the freed slaves were sent out of state. If a free black person was found promoting abolition in Maryland, he could be jailed for 10 to 20 years.

Under pressure from the slave states, the federal government also tightened controls on slaves. In 1850, Congress passed a law that made it more difficult for runaway slaves to evade capture. The Fugitive Slave Act was part of a set of new laws called the Compromise of 1850. The new laws were called a "compromise" because both proslavery and antislavery advocates got something they wanted. Antislavery lawmakers won the admission of California to the United States as a free state where slavery was not allowed. They also won passage of a law that banned the slave trade in Washington, D.C., the nation's capital. In return, proslavery lawmakers won the Fugitive Slave Act, a law that was despised by slaves, free blacks, and abolitionists.

The Fugitive Slave Act required the return of captured runaway slaves to their owners, no matter where those runaways were found. The law allowed slave owners to pursue runaway slaves over state lines. Under the law, slaves who had escaped to a free state in the North had to be sent back to their owners in the South. Federal marshals who did not arrest runaway slaves faced large fines. Furthermore, a suspected runaway could be returned to any person who claimed ownership without a jury trial or the right of the runaway to testify on his or her own behalf. People suspected of aiding a runaway slave by providing food, money, or shelter could be imprisoned for six months and fined $1,000. Officers who captured runaway slaves could be paid a fee for such captures, a provision of the new law that led to the capture of free blacks. Only four lawmakers voted against the law. People in Northern states who did not approve of slavery now had to consent to the capture and return of fugitive slaves.

ABOLITIONIST FUROR

Abolitionists were furious about this law that forced them to support slavery. The abolitionist movement was started by Quakers in England to stop the slave trade between Europe, Africa, and the Americas. The movement had a victory in 1807 with the passage by the British Parliament of the Abolition of the Slave Trade Act. On August 1, 1834, all slaves in the British Empire, which included all the British colonies, were emancipated, or freed. Before the American Revolution, a similar movement was under way in the colonies that later became the

THE *NORTH STAR*

On December 3, 1847, the abolitionist and orator Frederick Douglass published the first issue of his newspaper, the *North Star*, in Rochester, New York. The title evoked the North Star of the sky, the star that served as both symbol and signpost to the North for runaway slaves. Douglass, too, had run away from slavery. Born a slave in Talbot County, Maryland, in 1818, he escaped to New York and then to New Bedford, Massachusetts. He heard the abolitionist William Lloyd Garrison speak, joined the movement, and soon became a popular speaker, writer, and advocate not only against slavery but also for women's rights. In 1835, he published his first autobiography, *Narrative of the Life of Frederick Douglass, An American Slave*. This excerpt is from the first issue of the *North Star*, whose motto was "Right is of no Sex—Truth is of no Color—God is the Father of us all, and we are all brethren."

It is neither a reflection on the fidelity, nor a disparagement of the ability of our friends and fellow-laborers, to assert what "common sense affirms and only folly denies," that the man who has suffered the wrong is the man to demand redress, —that the man STRUCK is the man to CRY OUT—and that he who has endured the cruel pangs of Slavery is the man to advocate Liberty. It is evident we must be our own representatives and advocates, not exclusively, but peculiarly—not distinct from, but in connection with our white friends. In the grand struggle for liberty and equality now waging, it is meet, right and essential that there should arise in our ranks authors and editors, as well as orators, for it is in these capacities that the most permanent good can be rendered to our cause.

United States. Quakers in Philadelphia pushed fellow Quakers who were slaveholders to free their slaves. In 1775, Quakers founded the first antislavery society in the colonies, the Society for the Relief of Free Negroes Unlawfully Held in Bondage. Later called the Pennsylvania Abolition Society, the group not only advocated the end of slavery, but also helped free blacks to gain jobs, education, and housing so that they could live as free men and women. Other abolitionist groups were started in Boston, New York, and more Northern cities.

By the 1830s, although more people were speaking out against slavery, they still were a small minority. Those who spoke out faced harsh criticism for saying that laws should be broken, even if, in the eyes of many people, the laws were unfair or immoral. Evangelical preachers such as Charles Grandison Finney gave emotional antislavery sermons from their pulpits on Sundays. Writers used pen and ink to spread their beliefs. On January 1, 1831, William Lloyd Garrison, the son of a sea captain from Massachusetts, published the first issue of his abolitionist newspaper, *The Liberator*. Garrison's famous call to join the abolitionist cause appeared in that first issue:

I am aware, that many object to the severity of my language; but is there not cause for severity? I will be as harsh as truth, and as uncompromising as justice. On this subject, I do not wish to think, or speak, or write with moderation. No! No! Tell a man whose house is on fire to give a moderate alarm; tell him to moderately rescue his wife from the hands of the ravisher; tell the mother to gradually extricate her babe from the fire into which it has fallen—but urge me not to use moderation in a cause like the present. I am in earnest—I will not equivocate—I will not excuse—I will not retreat a single inch—and I WILL BE HEARD!

Every week, from 1831 until 1865, Garrison's newspaper printed passionate arguments for the immediate freeing of all slaves. The circulation was never enormous, but the influence of Garrison and other abolitionists was strong.

The popular New England Quaker poet John Greenleaf Whittier used his lyrical talents to promote the abolitionist cause. In his 1846 poem "New Hampshire," he urged other states to follow the Granite State's example in abolishing slavery: "Courage, then, Northern hearts! Be firm, be true;/What one brave State hath done, can ye not also do?"

One of the most important antislavery writers was a Connecticut teacher named Harriet Beecher Stowe. In response to the Fugitive Slave Act she wrote *Uncle Tom's Cabin*, a powerful best-selling novel about a slave family that sought its freedom. In 1857, a free black man named Samuel Green in Dorchester County, Maryland, was found with a copy of Stowe's book. He was sentenced to 10 years in prison.

The abolitionist movement was also built by slaves and free blacks. In the years before the Civil War, the freed slave Sojourner Truth, who was born in about 1797, traveled from city to city speaking out against slavery. One of the most respected abolitionists was Frederick Douglass. He grew up in slavery not far from Tubman's birthplace. After his escape, first to New York and then to Massachusetts, Douglass became a leading aboli- tionist. He eventually settled in Rochester, in upstate New York. Douglass was a fiery and eloquent speaker and was admired by both blacks and whites. He attacked the Fugitive Slave Law in a speech that he delivered at a convention in Ithaca, New York, in 1852. He criticized the provision of the law that did not give the fugitive slave a right to a jury. "A man may not throw the noose of a rope over the horns of an ox without having his right to do so submitted to a jury; but he may seize, bind and chain a man—a being whose value is beyond all computation, and doom him to life-long bondage by a summary process," said Douglass. Douglass became a strong admirer of Tubman.

Douglass and the other abolitionists fought hard against the Fugitive Slave Act. Vigilance committees were organized in Northern cities to help runaways avoid capture. African-American churches opened their doors as safe houses. Those most affected by the law were, of course, the fugitives themselves. In 1851, in Lancaster County, Pennsylvania, a group of fugitive slaves from Maryland and their supporters fought back against a group of slave catchers. This incident, which became known as the Christiana Riot, resulted in the death of a slave owner. Using the literary form known as irony, Douglass later wrote a comment on the event in his newspaper: "Didn't they know that slavery, not freedom, is their natural condition? Didn't they know that their legs, arms, eyes, hands, and heads, were the rightful property of the white men who claimed them? . . . Oh! Ye naughty and rebellious fellows! Why stand ye up like men, after this might decree?"

A few years later, a young former slave named Anthony Burns was arrested in Boston under the Fugitive Slave Act. He was given a trial but then transported by armed marshals back to slavery in Virginia. In reaction to his case, riots broke out in Boston. This and other rebellions against the Fugitive Slave Act have been called the bloody dawn of the coming Civil War. For Tubman, the law was one more obstacle on her difficult journeys to freedom.

BOUND FOR THE PROMISED LAND

With the passage of the Fugitive Slave Act, Tubman's journeys on the Underground Railroad became even more dangerous. Philadelphia was not safe from slave catchers. Tubman had to lead her charges onward to New York, where she could get them onto northbound trains so that they could make it to true freedom in Canada.

Tubman's immediate challenge of getting slaves out of Maryland was difficult enough. She risked grave danger every time she went back home. Neither Maryland nor Delaware showed any tolerance to runaway slaves. Slave catchers patrolled the roads with whips and dogs. If Tubman were to be caught

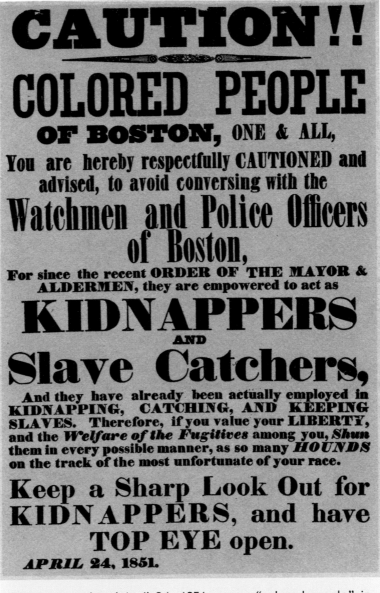

CAUTION!!

COLORED PEOPLE

OF BOSTON, ONE & ALL,

You are hereby respectfully CAUTIONED and advised, to avoid conversing with the

Watchmen and Police Officers of Boston,

For since the recent ORDER OF THE MAYOR & ALDERMEN, they are empowered to act as

KIDNAPPERS

AND

Slave Catchers,

And they have already been actually employed in KIDNAPPING, CATCHING, AND KEEPING SLAVES. Therefore, if you value your LIBERTY, and the *Welfare of the Fugitives* among you, *Shun* them in every possible manner, as so many *HOUNDS* on the track of the most unfortunate of your race.

Keep a Sharp Look Out for KIDNAPPERS, and have TOP EYE open.

APRIL 24, 1851.

This poster, dated April 24, 1851, warns "colored people" in Boston about policemen and others acting as slave catchers. The Fugitive Slave Act, passed in 1850, declared that all runaway slaves be returned to their masters. Besides the risk of punishment and even death if the fugitives were caught, many Northerners feared that free blacks would also be kidnapped and sold into slavery.

bringing others to freedom, she would suffer for it. She could be sold farther south, or punished harshly. Sometimes, runaway slaves were given hard labor. Despite the risks, Tubman left Philadelphia, heading south, in December 1850. She traveled to Baltimore, the capital city on the coast of Maryland, to rescue her niece, Kessiah, and Kessiah's two children. There she waited until Kessiah could escape.

Kessiah was the daughter of one of Tubman's sisters who had been sold South. Tubman planned the rescue with Kessiah's husband, John Bowley, who was a free black. Kessiah and her children were put on the auction block at the Eastern Shore Dorchester County courthouse. Bowley bid for them. When their owner went to lunch, however, Bowley helped them to escape. He got them to a boat on Cambridge Creek. They then went down the Choptank River to the Chesapeake Bay and from there sailed up to Baltimore, where Tubman met them.

For this rescue, Tubman must have had help from others on the Underground Railroad. Maryland had a small but strong Quaker population that was willing to help runaway slaves. Baltimore was not a city that was friendly to fugitive slaves, however. Any black person seen walking the streets had to be ready to show his or her papers. Tubman had forged papers that allowed the group to leave the city, and the fugitives made it to Philadelphia.

In the spring of 1851, Tubman dipped into her store of courage once again. This time, she rescued her brother Moses and two other men. The trip was successful, and Tubman's reputation grew as a skilled conductor on the Underground Railroad. By the fall of 1851, Tubman was ready to go back home to Dorchester County to get her husband, John. It was a difficult trek of nearly 100 miles. She probably hid by day and found her way through swamps and rivers and along back roads by night. When she arrived at John Tubman's cabin, however, she met with disappointment. With Harriet Tubman away in Philadelphia, John had found a new wife. She was a free black woman named Catherine. Harriet Tubman faced the unexpected truth that her marriage was finished. She was not the sort of person who let sorrow stop her from moving on, however. She still had to rescue the rest of her family and bring them to freedom.

CROSSING THE RIVER JORDAN

Amazingly, despite her repeated trips back to Maryland, Tubman was never caught. Nor did she ever lose one of her passengers. After her rescues became well known, Frederick Douglass wrote this about her: "Most of that I have done has been in public, and I have received much encouragement. . . . While the most that you have done has been witnessed by a few trembling, scared and foot sore bondsmen. . . . The midnight sky and the silent stars have been the witness of your devotion to freedom and your heroism."

People still wonder how Tubman did it. She often said that her strong religious faith helped guide her rescue missions. She was sure that what she was doing was right in the eyes of God. That faith and certainty gave Tubman the strength to attempt what few people would have dared. Here are the words of Underground Railroad stationmaster Thomas Garrett, in Bradford's book *Scenes in the Life of Harriet Tubman*:

> She has frequently told me that she talked with God, and he talked with her every day of her life, and she has declared to me that she felt no more fear of being arrested by her former master, or any other person, when in his immediate neighborhood, than she did in the State of New York, or Canada, for she said she never ventured only where God sent her, and her faith in a Supreme Power truly was great.

Garrett's home and hardware store in Wilmington, Delaware, were important havens for Tubman and her fugitives. He helped with food, money, and clothing for the runaways.

As much as her faith led her, so did her ingenuity and her tough-minded, practical nature. Often, her faith and practicality mingled. When a voice from God told her to lead two slaves into a river through which she had to wade with water up to her arms, she did so. Later, she found, the slave catchers were near. In 1903, the *New York Herald Tribune* printed this:

> On some darkly propitious night there would be breathed about the Negro quarters of a plantation word that she had come to lead them forth. At midnight, she would stand waiting in the depths of woodland or timbered swamp, and stealthily, one by one, her fugitives would creep to the rendezvous. She entrusted her plans to but few of the party. . . . She knew her path well by this time, and they followed her unerring guidance without question. She assumed the authority and enforced the discipline of a military despot.

Tubman did what was necessary to succeed. She paid bribes to people who could help her. She wore disguises, when necessary, to hide in plain sight when she went back home. During one trip back to Maryland, she wore a sunbonnet and carried chickens, a ploy that allowed her to walk right by her former master, undetected.

Tubman made her plans ahead of time. She contacted her abolitionist and freed black friends along the escape routes to let them know that she and her passengers were coming. As Larson explains, Tubman planned for slaves to sneak away on Saturdays because their owners would not notice that they were missing on Sundays, which were days of rest. Moreover, newspapers could not print notices about the runaways until Monday.

Tubman did not venture onto plantations. She sent messages for her followers to meet her a few miles away. That way, Tubman would not be caught. She traveled mostly at night, following the stars for direction, and mostly in winter, when the long nights gave her more time to travel. Sometimes, using her strong singing voice, Tubman sang songs to the fugitives. The spirituals, familiar to the escaping slaves, may have included codes to warn if dangers were near. Tubman also carried a pistol in her pocket, to use when all else failed. She did not hesitate to pull it out if one of her runaways wanted to turn back, thus jeopardizing the others.

A Home
of Her Own

One of Tubman's most daring and heartbreaking rescues occurred during the Christmas season in 1854. At that time, three of Tubman's brothers still lived in slavery in Maryland. The brothers had tried several times to get away. They may have even tried to negotiate for their freedom with their owner, Eliza Ann Brodess, but their attempts had not succeeded. As the year neared its end, they suspected that they might be sold. For slaves, this prospect was terrifying. They could be torn away from their families forever and forced to live under the ownership of a stranger. Somehow, Tubman got word that her brothers needed her help. In late December, she arrived back in Maryland to rescue Henry, Robert, and Ben.

Because slaves often were given a day off for Christmas, the holiday was a good time to escape. A slave owner would not realize for a day or two that a slave had gone missing. Tubman probably arrived by boat on the banks of the Choptank River, perhaps after having traveled through Baltimore and getting help from abolitionists along the way. The brothers and several other slaves, including a woman, were waiting for Tubman near Ben Ross and Rittia Green's cabin. As Tubman's mother prepared food for Christmas, the fugitives hid in a small out-building, waiting for the safest time to get away.

Tubman had not seen her mother in six years and had missed her terribly. She did not dare to let the older woman know she was nearby, however. The less Rittia knew, the better; such dangerous knowledge about the location of her fugitive daughter could get the older woman in trouble. Tubman's father knew that his children were hiding, but he didn't dare look at them. That way, if he was questioned later, he could say, truthfully, that he had not seen them. Ben was able to push food to the group through the cabin door, however.

The group waited until a dark, rainy night to leave. According to later accounts, the escape took place on Christmas. The wife of one of Tubman's brothers was in labor, ready to have a baby. Her husband had to take this chance to flee, however, even if it meant leaving wife and baby behind. He would try to return for them later. As the group began its dangerous journey, Ben Ross tied a handkerchief around his eyes so that he didn't see the escape. He accompanied his children a little way down the road. Finally, they had to say good-bye. "The time of parting came, and they bade him farewell, and left him standing in the middle of the road. When he could no longer hear their footsteps he turned back, and taking the handkerchief from his eyes, he hastened home." So wrote Sarah Bradford, in *Harriet, The Moses of Her People.*

Before Tubman and her brothers left, they caught sight of their mother through the window of the cabin. Rittia didn't know that her children were close by outside and could see her. She looked upset, as if she already wondered where her sons had gone: Had they been sold South, or had they fled to freedom? She didn't know, wrote Bradford. Ben and Rittia later were asked whether they had seen their sons escape. "Old Ben says that he hasn't seen one of his children this Christmas," was their answer. They were telling the truth.

Slave hunters went looking for the runaways. The group may have stopped in Wilmington, at Thomas Garrett's house. In a letter dated December 29, 1854, Garrett wrote:

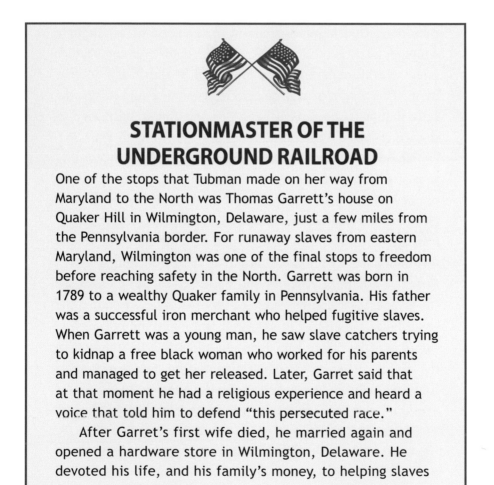

STATIONMASTER OF THE UNDERGROUND RAILROAD

One of the stops that Tubman made on her way from Maryland to the North was Thomas Garrett's house on Quaker Hill in Wilmington, Delaware, just a few miles from the Pennsylvania border. For runaway slaves from eastern Maryland, Wilmington was one of the final stops to freedom before reaching safety in the North. Garrett was born in 1789 to a wealthy Quaker family in Pennsylvania. His father was a successful iron merchant who helped fugitive slaves. When Garrett was a young man, he saw slave catchers trying to kidnap a free black woman who worked for his parents and managed to get her released. Later, Garret said that at that moment he had a religious experience and heard a voice that told him to defend "this persecuted race."

After Garret's first wife died, he married again and opened a hardware store in Wilmington, Delaware. He devoted his life, and his family's money, to helping slaves

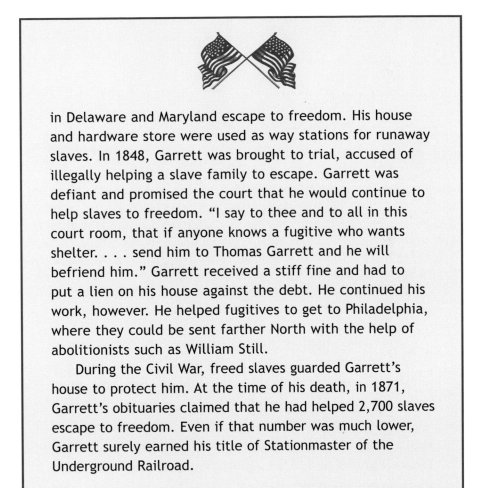

Esteemed Friend, J. Miller McKim: —We made arrangements last night, and sent away Harriet Tubman, with six men and one woman to Allen Agnew's, to be forwarded across the country to the city. Harriet, and one of the men had worn the shoes off their feet, and I gave them two dollars to help fit them out, and directed a carriage to be hired at my expense, to take them out, but do not yet know the expense.

THOMAS GARRETT

in Delaware and Maryland escape to freedom. His house and hardware store were used as way stations for runaway slaves. In 1848, Garrett was brought to trial, accused of illegally helping a slave family to escape. Garrett was defiant and promised the court that he would continue to help slaves to freedom. "I say to thee and to all in this court room, that if anyone knows a fugitive who wants shelter. . . . send him to Thomas Garrett and he will befriend him." Garrett received a stiff fine and had to put a lien on his house against the debt. He continued his work, however. He helped fugitives to get to Philadelphia, where they could be sent farther North with the help of abolitionists such as William Still.

During the Civil War, freed slaves guarded Garrett's house to protect him. At the time of his death, in 1871, Garrett's obituaries claimed that he had helped 2,700 slaves escape to freedom. Even if that number was much lower, Garrett surely earned his title of Stationmaster of the Underground Railroad.

About 1,000 slaves each year managed to flee to the North, although many more tried unsuccessfully. Fugitives traveled alone or in small groups at night, in intense weather, and preferably in the rain because the storm could cover their tracks. Escapees slept in the woods, in haystacks, or in caves, and like Tubman, they learned to follow the North Star in a zig-zag pattern.

Like many fugitive slaves, Tubman's brothers changed their names when they got to Philadelphia. Ben took the name James Stewart; Robert became John Stewart; and Henry became William Henry Stewart. They chose the name Stewart from the wealthy Dorchester County family that had employed their family. The brothers met with William Still of the Underground Railroad, who took down their stories and gave them money to get to New York. There, they could take a train farther north.

The group eventually found its way to Ontario, Canada. Crossing the bridge over Niagara Falls was the final passage to freedom for many runaway slaves. Canada was a popular destination because the Fugitive Slave Act did not apply beyond the borders of the United States. Once safely on Canadian soil, runaways no longer had to live in fear of slave catchers or worry that they could be taken back to slavery. In Ontario, Tubman's brothers settled in St. Catharines and Chatham, 140 miles west, in an area that had a large fugitive slave community. A later photo of William Henry Stewart shows a slender, serious man in a suit. He looks nothing like a field hand.

At least one of Tubman's brothers may not have made it to freedom. It is not known what became of the youngest brother, Moses. He may have been sold South, or he may have died. In a strange coincidence, Tubman's nickname was her brother's name.

A SIMPLE BUGGY

Tubman's parents remained in Maryland, living in the cabin in Caroline County, where they worked for the Thompson family. Their situation had changed in some ways. Ben Ross had been freed by his owner, but the old couple had to put up with the humiliations of a slave society. Rittia Green was supposed to have been freed years earlier, but that had not happened. Ross finally was able to purchase his wife's freedom. On June 1, 1855, the local courthouse registered a payment of $20 by Ross to buy his wife's freedom from Eliza Ann Brodess. After a lifetime of slavery, Rittia Green was legally free. She was about 70 years old.

The couple still was subject to white employers, however, and still lived in fear. Like his daughter in Philadelphia, Ross had become an antislavery activist, helping other slaves to escape to freedom on the Underground Railroad. In March 1857, Ross sheltered a group of runaway slaves in his cabin. His activities became known to local authorities. Fearing arrest, Ross made preparations to get away—out of Maryland and out of the South.

Knowing that her parents were in trouble, Tubman headed back home. The early spring was cold that year, and the journey was rough. This time, she took more risks than usual. Although early biographies of Tubman claim that a $40,000 bounty was offered for her capture, there may not have been a price on her head. If there was, it may have been about $1,200. In any case, although the authorities probably suspected that someone was responsible for the escape of many slaves, they did not know the name of the person for sure. Tubman still had to be careful.

When she arrived in Caroline County and neared her parents' home, Tubman got a horse and used ropes, boards, and wheels to build a simple buggy. Her parents were too old to walk all the way to freedom. Even with the buggy all ready for them, her parents were reluctant to leave their possessions behind. They knew they had to go, however. Tubman got them to Delaware, to her friend Thomas Garrett in Wilmington. Garrett gave Tubman $30 for her parents' journey, and the three traveled on to Philadelphia. There, the old couple told their story of slavery to William Still, whose collection of stories of runaway slaves was growing rapidly. They described their difficult lives, and told how they still mourned for their children who had been sold South. After a short rest, Tubman and her parents went on to New York City and then to Rochester, in upstate New York. Quaker families let them stay in their homes in both cities. Finally, Tubman led her parents over the Canadian border to Ontario, where her brothers and their families were living. At last, most of the family was united in freedom.

HOME AT LAST

In 1859, Tubman moved her parents to Auburn, a small town in the Finger Lakes region of upstate New York. Slavery had been abolished in New York in 1827, and many free blacks had settled in and around Auburn, in Cayuga County. A number

THE *DRED SCOTT* DECISION, 1857

Dred Scott was born a slave in Missouri. His master, Dr. John Emerson, an army surgeon, took him to the free state of Illinois, and then to the territory of Wisconsin, which also had no slavery. When Emerson was ordered to return to Missouri, he brought Scott with him. Back in Missouri, Scott and his wife were hired out to work. After Emerson's death, Scott sought his freedom. After all, he had lived as a free man in Illinois and Wisconsin. When Emerson's widow refused to buy his freedom, Scott hired lawyers to sue for his freedom. The case went all the way to the United States Supreme Court.

In 1857, in the landmark decision *Dred Scott v. Sandford*, the court ruled that slaves and the descendants of slaves were not, and never could be, U.S. citizens. The justices said that the drafters of the Constitution considered African Americans to be "beings of an inferior order, and altogether unfit to associate with the white race, either in social or political relations, and so far inferior that they had no rights which the white man was bound to respect." Furthermore, because they were not citizens, African Americans could not sue in the courts.

A divided Court, split 7 to 5, also ruled that Congress could not ban slavery in the federal territories in which westward-moving pioneers were settling. The Missouri Compromise of 1850, which prohibited slavery in certain territories, was now unconstitutional. The justices said that the compromise violated the Fifth Amendment, which prohibits Congress from taking property from people without due process of law.

(continues)

(continued)

Southerners who favored slavery applauded the *Dred Scott* decision. They agreed that Congress should not be able to ban slavery in the territories, and that slaves should not have the rights of citizens. For slaves and abolitionists, the *Dred Scott* case was a terrible setback because it seemed to open the gates to the admission of even more slave states to the Union. One Midwestern legislator was particularly outraged. A Republican lawyer and political activist in Illinois named Abraham Lincoln expressed disgust at the ruling.

In a speech in Springfield, Illinois, on June 26, 1857, Lincoln pointed out that the Founding Fathers who had written the Declaration of Independence had said that "all men are created equal." By the 1850s, black men were able to vote in five states. Now, however, that basic citizen's right was denied to black men. Although Lincoln was not in favor of African Americans and whites marrying—a fear that loomed over the *Dred Scott* case—he believed that African Americans should be given basic rights and respect. Speaking of an African-American woman, he said, "In some respects she certainly is not my equal; but in her natural

of Quaker abolitionists also lived in the rural county, which was dotted with small towns tucked here and there in the rolling farmland. The free blacks and abolitionists published antislavery newspapers, petitioned Congress to end slavery, raised money for antislavery lectures, and opened their homes to fugitives heading northward to Canada. Because the village of Auburn was considered a crossroads on the Underground

right to eat the bread she earns with her own hands without asking leave of any one else, she is my equal, and the equal of all others."

Lincoln also spoke about the differences between pro-slavery Democrats and anti-slavery Republicans:

> Republicans inculcate, with whatever of ability—they can, that the negro is a man; that his bondage is cruelly wrong, and that the field of his oppression ought not to be enlarged. The Democrats deny his manhood; deny, or dwarf to insignificance, the wrong of his bondage; so far as possible, crush all sympathy for him, and cultivate and excite hatred and disgust against him; compliment themselves as Union-savers for doing so; and call the indefinite outspreading of his bondage "a sacred right of self-government."

For Lincoln and many others, the *Dred Scott* decision sharpened the divide between Democrats and Republicans, and between the South and the North. Three years later, Lincoln was elected president; the following year, the Civil War began. As for Scott, his former master's son purchased him and his wife, and set them free.

Railroad, it is not surprising that Tubman chose it to be her new home.

Once again, the kindness of strangers gave Tubman a chance for a better future. William Henry Seward let Harriet stay in a two-story brick house on South Street, at the edge of Auburn. A leading abolitionist, Seward was also a New York state senator. He already had served as governor of New York and later

William Seward *(above)*, American statesman and secretary of state under presidents Abraham Lincoln and Andrew Johnson became a radical opponent of slavery after traveling through the South and observing slave conditions. He presented himself as the enemy of slave power and defended runaway slaves in court.

became secretary of state under President Abraham Lincoln. In December 1865, Seward officially proclaimed the end of slavery with the ratification of the Thirteenth Amendment to the Constitution.

In the years before the Civil War, Seward and his wife Frances let fugitive slaves stay in their home. In 1859, Seward sold the house and small farm to Tubman, although he may not ever have collected the money. Some researchers believe this was an illegal transaction. Two years earlier, in the *Dred Scott* decision, the U.S. Supreme Court had declared that blacks were not citizens. This meant that blacks could not sign legal contracts. In any case, thanks to this transaction, Tubman had a home of her own. Generous as always, she opened it up to anyone who needed shelter. In the coming years, her family from Maryland settled nearby, and she was surrounded by her loved ones.

JOHN BROWN'S RAID

The antislavery movement was heating up. A dramatic antislavery action was about to take place, and Tubman knew all about it. When she was in St. Catharines, Ontario, in the spring of 1858, she met a man named John Brown. Brown was a militant abolitionist who was prepared to use violence to end slavery. He even dreamed of founding a new, interracial country with its own constitution. Frederick Douglass knew Brown and commented, "though a white gentleman, [he] is in sympathy a black man, and as deeply interested in our cause, as though his own soul had been pierced with the iron of slavery." Brown told Douglass that he wanted to start a war to end slavery.

Brown deeply admired Tubman. He called her "General Tubman" for her brave work leading slaves to freedom. Brown considered her a partner, as strong as a man; he called her "the most of a man naturally that I have ever met." Although she had never supported the use of violence, Tubman fell in behind Brown. He paid her to recruit followers, and she may have advised him on tactics and geography. Political events spurred Brown on. The Kansas-Nebraska Act of 1854 allowed the settlers in those territories to decide whether to allow slavery when they applied for statehood. This new law overturned the Missouri Compromise, which banned slavery in the

Abolitionist John Brown once called Harriet Tubman "one of the bravest persons on this continent." Tubman helped to raise money for Brown's raid at Harpers Ferry, Virginia. Brown and his men were captured by Colonel Robert E. Lee's militiamen, and Brown was hanged. In 1912, in one of Tubman's last interviews, she continued to refer to him as "my dearest friend."

two territories. Brown went west with his sons and attacked proslavery settlers in Kansas and Missouri. He was planning something even bigger, however. From 1858 through 1859,

Tubman met with Brown and gave talks and speeches to raise funds for his cause.

Tubman was not nearby when, on October 16, 1859, Brown and 21 men sneaked into the small town of Harpers Ferry, Virginia. According to different sources, Tubman may have been in Massachusetts or New York. Brown was determined to incite a slave uprising and rebellion that would put an end to slavery. The residents of the town were sleeping when Brown and his band of five blacks and 14 to 16 whites broke into their homes. The raiders took 60 local people hostage and occupied the town's federal arsenal and rifle works. Brown hoped to arm slaves with the guns and ammunition. Brown's raid was a disaster. Farmers, militiamen, and soldiers led by Colonel Robert E. Lee moved in quickly. In less than two days, Brown's men were almost all killed or captured, and the uprising was put down. Lee went on to become the leading general of the Southern forces during the Civil War.

Brown was put on trial and convicted of treason. He maintained that what he had done was right. At his sentencing, Brown said, "Now, if it be deemed necessary that I should forfeit my life for the furtherance of the ends of justice, and mingle my blood further with the blood of my children, and with the blood of millions in this slave country whose rights are disregarded by wicked, cruel, and unjust enactments, I submit: so let it be done."

Brown was hanged on December 2, 1859. Some people in the North who agreed that slavery was wrong came to admire Brown, though not his violent methods. The Massachusetts writer Henry David Thoreau said of Brown: "No man in America has ever stood up so persistently and effectively for the dignity of human nature."

THE RESCUE OF CHARLES NALLE

In the spring of 1860, Tubman made one of her boldest rescues. It did not happen below the Mason-Dixon Line that separated the South from the North and did not take place in the dead of night. Charles Nalle was a fugitive slave who escaped from his owner in Virginia and fled to New York State. He found his way to Troy, New York, where he lived in the home of a black grocer. Nalle's owner was looking for him and had a legal right, under the 1850 Fugitive Slave Act, to bring him back to Virginia. Soon, he caught up with Nalle. On April 17, 1860, Nalle was on his way to a bakery when a U.S. deputy marshal and a slave catcher from Virginia, hired by Nalle's owner, arrested him. Nalle was brought to the U.S. commissioner's office. A wagon was ready outside to take him back to Virginia.

Crowds of local abolitionists gathered to prevent Nalle from being taken South. Tubman was on her way to Boston that day, and she happened to stop in Troy to visit a cousin. After hearing what was happening, she went to the commissioner's office. There, she pushed her way upstairs to the room where Nalle was being held. She wore a sunbonnet and shawl and carried a food basket. She appeared to be a harmless, elderly woman. According to some accounts, people outside the building could see Tubman's sunbonnet through the window. "There stands Old Moses yet, and as long as she is there, he is safe," they said, according to Sarah Bradford.

Tubman told some small boys to say that there was a fire, to spark panic in the crowd. The arresting officers tried to get Nalle down the stairs, but Tubman, pretending to be a very old woman, would not move out the way. Some in the crowd called out that they would pay for Nalle's freedom.

When one of the men guarding Nalle agreed to a price, the guards started to bring the prisoner down the stairs to take him outside. Tubman shouted out and grabbed at the officers. She took off her bonnet and tied it on Nalle to confuse the crowd and the police. She kept her hold on Nalle and dragged him out of the building. She took him to the nearby river and got him onto a ferry. Tubman also boarded a ferry. On the other side of the river, however, Nalle was captured. When Tubman found out where he was, she hurried to reach him. Several men had been shot. Tubman rushed through the crowd and, once again, dragged Nalle away. Somehow, this time, he was able to make it out of town to freedom.

LAST RIDE

The leaves had fallen from the trees and the first frosts were hardening the ground in November 1860, when Tubman left Auburn to make her last journey on the Underground Railroad. She was hoping to rescue her sister Rachel and Rachel's children, Ben and Angerine. Tubman made her way back to Dorchester County, Maryland. Once there, she learned that Rachel had died. Tubman was unable to bring back the children, possibly because she could not afford to pay a bribe for them. Historians have not found out what happened to Ben and Angerine. They probably remained in slavery.

Tubman was able to lead away another group of escaping slaves, however. This band of passengers included the Ennals family, who had two or three children and a tiny baby. The trip North was risky because of the slave catchers who patrolled the roads. The family members had to separate. Tubman crisscrossed the countryside, seeking help from black families and Quakers. Once, she knocked on the door of a black family only to find a white man in the house. At one point, she led the mother and children of the Ennals family as they waded across a cold river to camp overnight on a swampy island. They slept on a quilt on the frozen ground. Tubman helped carry the baby in a basket and gave it a drug to make it sleep so that it would not cry. When Tubman got separated from the group as she looked for food or shelter, she whistled or sang a hymn, and the others answered.

By the time Tubman and her passengers finally reached Auburn, at the end of December, the weather was bitterly cold, and the group was nearly starving. An abolitionist couple, David and Martha Wright, opened their homes to the fugitives. Martha Wright was the younger sister of Lucretia Mott and had been educated in Quaker schools. She was also a friend of Tubman's. The Wrights' home was a frequent stop on the Underground Railroad. Although Martha was eager to help fugitive slaves, her family was more cautious.

In an 1848 letter to her sister Lucretia, Martha Wright described the stay of one runaway slave. Martha's children did not like having the fugitive in their house, and her husband locked the door to the kitchen, where the man stayed the night by the stove. David Wright said that if the slave's owner came for him, he would "not defend him." The letter shows how families were torn by the risks they took to help slaves to freedom.

This time, Martha Wright wrote another letter. It was dated December 30, 1860: "We have been extending our sympathies, as well as congratulations, on seven newly arrived slaves that Harriet Tubman has just pioneered safely from the Southern Part of Maryland. One woman carried a baby all the way and brought two other children that Harriet and the men helped a long."

On this last journey, Tubman took the Ennals family all the way to Canada. In all, Tubman made 12 or 13 trips on the Underground Railroad. According to the most recent estimates, she led about 70 people to freedom, including the members of her own family. Through all kinds of weather and in all sorts of circumstances, Tubman put her life at risk in the name of freedom. During the late 1850s, Tubman told her story and the story of the Underground Railroad at antislavery rallies. When fellow abolitionist Thomas Higginson introduced her to a crowd in Worcester, Massachusetts, in 1859, he introduced her as "Moses," a name that has stuck, even until today. Tubman once said that her friend William Lloyd Garrison gave her the nickname. Whoever first bestowed it, the name "Moses" was fitting. Just as Moses led the Israelites to the promised land, so did Tubman lead her own people to freedom.

5

Nurse and Spy

The election of President Abraham Lincoln in November 1860 was not welcomed by slaveholders in the South. Lincoln was a member of the antislavery Republican Party. He had often expressed his hatred of slavery. "Those who deny freedom to others, deserve it not for themselves; and, under a just God, can not long retain it," he said in 1858. Lincoln believed that slavery was wrong, and he did not want it to expand into new states and territories. Still, although he would later change his mind, at the time of his election, Lincoln did not propose the immediate emancipation of slaves or the abolishment of slavery in the South. Instead, he thought that slavery eventually would fade away naturally. Southerners, however, believed that Lincoln's presidency would harm the rights of individual states to govern themselves and to determine their own economies.

Tubman did not believe Abraham Lincoln could beat the South until he freed the slaves. When Lincoln finally put the Emancipation Proclamation into effect in January 1863, which she thought was an important first step, she renewed her support for war by guiding Union troops on armed raids.

The Southern states wanted no part of the United States of America if Lincoln was to be its leader. On December 20, 1860, South Carolina declared that it would secede, or withdraw, from the Union. This was a drastic move because it would break the nation apart. By February 1861, six more states had joined South Carolina in secession. In that month, representatives from South Carolina, Georgia, Florida, Louisiana, Alabama, and Mississippi gathered in Montgomery, Alabama, to form the Confederate States of America. Texas seceded in February.

The Confederate representatives elected Jefferson Davis as president of the Confederacy. A short, slight man with a reputation for stubbornness, Davis owned a cotton plantation in Mississippi. He had served as secretary of war under President Franklin Pierce and represented Mississippi in the U.S. Senate. In his first inaugural address, in February 1861, Jefferson said that "necessity, not choice" had caused the secession of the Southern states. He also said:

> Our present condition, achieved in a manner unprecedented in the history of nations, illustrates the American idea that governments rest upon the consent of the governed, and that it is the right of the people to alter or abolish governments whenever they become destructive of the ends for which they were established.

A few weeks later, on March 4, President Lincoln delivered his inaugural address in Washington, D.C. He expressed his disapproval of the new Confederate states. He believed that the secessions were illegal and would lead to civil war, and he was prepared to defend the Union. He did not plan to invade the South or to abolish slavery, but he was willing to use force to keep the country united. He pleaded with the Southern states to restore the Union. Speaking to the South, he said, "In your hands, my dissatisfied fellow countrymen, and not in mine, is the momentous issue of civil war. The government will not assail you. . . . You have no oath registered in Heaven to destroy the government, while I shall have the most solemn one to preserve, protect and defend it."

On April 12, 1861, South Carolinian soldiers fired on Fort Sumter, a federal fort in Charleston Harbor. After 34 hours of bombardment, Fort Sumter surrendered to the Southern troops. In quick response, Lincoln called for volunteers to form a militia of 75,000 to fight against the South. Already, many Northern states had started to call up soldiers. Soon, four more slave states joined the Confederacy, while four others remained within the Union. The American Civil War had begun.

"UNDER THE SUPERVISION OF A SUPERIOR RACE"

On April 29, 1861, Jefferson Davis spoke to the Provisional Congress of the Confederate States of America, which was meeting in Montgomery, Alabama. He explained why the South had seceded from the Union and that the Southern economy relied on slaves.

In the meantime, under the mild and genial climate of the Southern States and the increasing care and attention for the well-being and comfort of the laboring class, dictated alike by interest and humanity, the African slaves had augmented in number from about 600,000, at the date of the adoption of the constitutional compact, to upward of 4,000,000. In moral and social condition they had been elevated from brutal savages into docile, intelligent, and civilized agricultural laborers, and supplied

JOINING THE UNION EFFORT

Like other abolitionists, Tubman was frustrated that Lincoln did not immediately put an end to slavery. She was horrified that, when slaves fled to Union strongholds in the Confederacy during the early months of the war, Lincoln still was reluctant to free them immediately. "God won't let master Lincoln beat the South till he does *the right thing*," Tubman declared. Still, Tubman told a friend that she had a vision that slaves would soon be free. Although blacks and women were not allowed to enlist in the army, Tubman was determined to help the United States. She set out to raise funds for the war effort. By this time,

not only with bodily comforts but with careful religious instruction. Under the supervision of a superior race their labor had been so directed as not only to allow a gradual and marked amelioration of their own condition, but to convert hundreds of thousands of square miles of wilderness into cultivated lands covered with a prosperous people; towns and cities had sprung into existence, and had rapidly increased in wealth and population under the social system of the South; the white population of the Southern slaveholding States had augmented form about 1,250,000 at the date of the adoption of the Constitution to more than 8,500,000 in 1860; and the productions of the South in cotton, rice, sugar, and tobacco, for the full development and continuance of which the labor of African slaves was and is indispensable, had swollen to an amount which formed nearly three-fourths of the exports of the whole United States and had become absolutely necessary to the wants of civilized man.

Tubman's fame had grown. People throughout the country compared her to Moses, who had led his people out of Egypt to freedom. She knew many leading citizens in Boston, New York, and Philadelphia. Through them, she was able to become more involved in the war.

An early Tubman biographer, Earl Conrad, wrote that Tubman joined General Benjamin Butler from Massachusetts in May 1861, but this is not certain. Butler's troops headed to Fort Monroe in Virginia, at the mouth of the James River, on the Chesapeake Bay. Butler declared that slaves escaping to Fort Monroe would not be returned to their owners. As the months of fighting progressed, runaway slaves from the states of the Confederacy found shelter at Fort Monroe, earning it the nickname "Freedom's Fortress." Thousands of fugitives made their way to safety there.

In the view of the federal government, these runaways were considered contraband—property seized from the enemy that could be put to work without pay. The runaways might, however, be paid for their work at a later time. The men worked as manual laborers; the women helped to wash soldiers' clothes and prepare meals. In Conrad's account, Tubman helped the runaways with her nursing and cooking skills. More recent biographers are unsure that she took this trip, however.

Through her abolitionist friends, Tubman met the governor of Massachusetts, John Andrew, who was strongly against slavery. Governor Andrew admired Tubman and arranged for her to join Quaker volunteers who were heading into the Confederacy to help the fugitive slaves gathered on the coast of South Carolina and on the Sea Islands. This region was deep in slaveholding territory, and Tubman was taking a big risk to go there. As Catherine Clinton notes in her biography, "she was still a wanted woman in the slave South." Tubman's trip was sponsored by the New England Freedmen's Aid Society. Her Boston friends and other abolitionists raised money to pay her way. Before she left for the South, she may have gone back to

Pictured, a group of escaped slaves outside a cabin. Benjamin Butler announced that any slaves on land controlled by the Union was to be considered contraband property. He refused to return any escaped slaves to their owners if they had come within Fort Monroe. Seen as a step in the direction of gaining freedom, an estimated 10,000 escaped slaves found their way to Fort Monroe requesting they be considered contraband.

upstate New York to see her parents, to make sure that they had enough money.

PIES, GINGER BREAD, AND ROOT BEER

In May 1862, the federal ship *Atlantic* anchored at Beaufort, on Port Royal Bay in South Carolina. The previous fall, ships of the Union Navy had attacked Confederate forts on Hilton Head Island, one of the Sea Islands. The Confederate troops fell back, and the Union Army set up headquarters on the island. Known as the Department of the South, the headquarters were nominally in charge of South Carolina, Florida, and Georgia during the war. Slaves from coastal rice, cotton, and indigo plantations found sanctuary at the Union stronghold. When Tubman arrived, the island's docks were crowded with freed slaves. Impoverished and with no means to support themselves, some of the refugees wore nothing but gunnysacks. Tubman could barely understand their speech because many of them spoke the part-African dialect of the Sea Islands known as Gullah. The Northern abolitionists hoped to help these former slaves learn skills so that they could support themselves as free men and women.

Tubman went to work at a house set up by the Young Men's Christian Association—the YMCA. She organized the freed-women to cook, wash, and clean for the Union soldiers. Both blacks and whites called her "Moses." Many of the soldiers knew who she was, and they tipped their caps in respect to her. At first, she took government food rations for herself. When she saw how hungry the freed slaves were, however, she felt uncomfortable about using up the limited resources. Instead, she began to earn money by selling pies, ginger bread, and root beer that she made herself. She sent some of her earnings home to her family in New York.

Tubman also was called on to nurse the soldiers and the freed slaves. In the swampy heat of the South Carolina coast, diseases such as malaria, typhoid, cholera, typhus, and dysentery were common. Mosquitoes, ticks, and other insects carried diseases as well. Doctors had no antibiotics to stop infection and no antiseptics to clean wounds. Tubman described her nursing efforts to Sarah Bradford. She explained that she put a big chunk of ice in a basin and filled the basin with water. When each wounded man arrived, she took a sponge, waved away the flies, and bathed the man's wounds. The water warmed up quickly, however, and turned red with blood. The flies soon returned.

When she was growing up in Maryland, Tubman learned how to use the roots of various plants to treat many illnesses. On Hilton Head, she found local plants that seemed to help her patients. At times, Tubman was called on to treat smallpox, a disease with no cure. She was considered by many to have a special power to heal the sick. One Union general even let her have bourbon whiskey to help ease the pain of her patients.

THE EMANCIPATION PROCLAMATION

On September 17, 1862, the Union Army won a major victory. The federal force turned back Confederate general Robert E. Lee's troops at Antietam Creek in Maryland, thereby preventing the Confederates from advancing into Union territory. This battle on the fields of Maryland was the bloodiest in American history. About 23,000 soldiers from both sides were killed. One soldier later wrote that the field "was so full of bodies that a man could have walked through it without stepping on the ground."

On the heels of this hard-won victory, Lincoln wrote a preliminary draft of the Emancipation Proclamation, a decree through which Lincoln planned to free the slaves in the Confederacy. The president had presented this idea to his generals a few months earlier. If the Confederate states did not rejoin the Union by January 1, 1863, the slaves in those states would be "forever free." Lincoln did not believe that he had the Constitutional power, as president, to abolish slavery. As commander in chief of the Union Army, however, he could abolish slavery in the Confederacy, where slaves helped with the war effort by digging ditches, tilling fields, and performing other tasks for their masters.

Lincoln signed his final version of the Emancipation Proclamation on January 1, 1863. The proclamation allowed

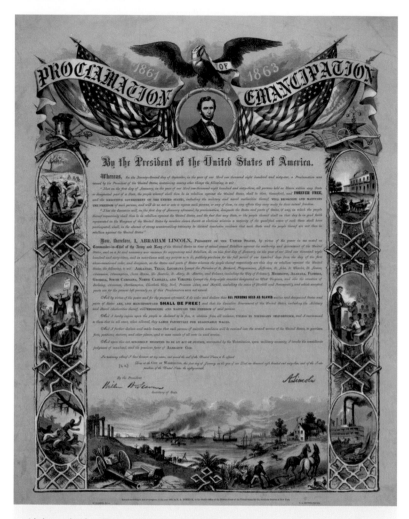

Although the Emancipation Proclamation did not free any slaves in the Southern states under Union control or the border states (Kentucky, Missouri, Maryland, Delaware, and West Virginia), thousands of slaves were freed each day as the Union Army defeated the Confederacy. Even after the passage of the proclamation, slavery continued to exist until the ratification of the Thirteenth Amendment on December 18, 1865.

the Union Army to enforce the freedom of slaves in the states of the Confederacy. Under the terms of the proclamation, freed blacks also were permitted to join the Union Army and Navy.

About 200,000 black troops fought in the Civil War, and 35,000 died in combat.

According to the Emancipation Proclamation, slave states that had not seceded from the Union could continue to practice slavery. Thus, slavery persisted, at least for the present, in Tubman's home state of Maryland. As for the Confederate states, they did not recognize Lincoln or his proclamation. It was apparent, now, that Lincoln planned, not only to win the war and reunite the South and the North, but also to abolish slavery across the land. In the months that followed, Lincoln's words against slavery became stronger. He had sown the seeds for what finally was accomplished in 1865, through the Thirteenth Amendment to the Constitution: the abolition and prohibition of slavery in all states.

SPY BEHIND THE LINES

Tubman found that her experiences on the Underground Railroad proved valuable to the war effort. Her abilities to track through the woods, disguise herself, and lead others on secret missions equipped her well to help carry on activities behind enemy lines. The Union Army turned to former slaves and free blacks to supply intelligence during the war. The military authorities called such information "Black Dispatches." According to the Central Intelligence Agency's Center for the Study of Intelligence, these dispatches were "the single most prolific and productive category of intelligence obtained and acted upon by Union forces throughout the Civil War." At the height of the war, in 1862, the abolitionist Frederick Douglass wrote this about the Union's black spies: "Negroes have repeatedly threaded their way through the lines of the rebels exposing themselves to bullets to convey important information to the loyal army of the Potomac."

Tubman worked under Colonel James Montgomery, a Union officer who led the 2nd South Carolina Volunteers. The Volunteers was a black army unit that conducted surprise attacks behind enemy lines. Tubman led spying trips into Confederate territory. She brought back information about troop movements and strengths. In January 1863, according to Kate Clifford Larson, Tubman was paid $100 for her spying efforts and to bribe informants. Tubman, in turn, paid local slaves and free blacks who knew the region and could help her with her operations. Dressed as a field hand or a farm wife, Tubman was not recognizable when she went on her missions.

A brief word portrait by historian Benjamin Quarles, in his book *The Negro in the Civil War*, brings Tubman to life in one of her many roles. Quarles writes:

> As a scout, Mrs. Harriet's deceptive appearance was a great asset. Who would have thought that this short, gnarled black woman with a bandanna wrapped around her head was engaged in such a bold venture as entering Rebel-held territory for the purposes of urging slaves to take to their heels, appraising military and naval defenses, and taking in with a knowing eye the location and quantity of supplies, provisions and livestock?

Also according to Quarles, the head of the volunteers, Rufus Saxton, wrote that Tubman "made many a raid inside the enemy's lines, displaying remarkable courage, zeal and fidelity."

In June 1863, Colonel Montgomery asked Tubman to help guide soldiers up South Carolina's Combahee River. The narrow, blackwater river was bordered by rice plantations and swamps and emptied into the Saint Helena Sound near Beaufort. Tubman was to lead the soldiers past the Confederate lines. As the sun set on June 2, Tubman guided Colonel Montgomery and 150 soldiers along the river and past the Confederate lines. The Union soldiers then surprised the Confederates and destroyed Confederate supplies.

The successful Union force brought back 700 to 800 slaves who were laborers on nearby plantations, as well as much enemy property. This feat made Tubman famous. *The*

HARRIET TUBMAN.

Pictured is Harriet Tubman in her Civil War clothing. In 1863, during the Civil War, Tubman became the first woman to lead an armed assault. Not only did she serve as a spy for the Union forces, a nurse to wounded soldiers, and a cook, she was praised for her recruiting efforts. Most of the newly liberated blacks joined the Union Army.

Commonwealth, a Boston newspaper, published a story about Tubman on July 10, 1863:

> Col. Montgomery and his gallant band of 800 black soldiers, under the guidance of a black woman, dashed in to the enemies' country . . . destroying millions of dollars worth of commissary stores, cotton and lordly dwellings, and striking terror to the heart of rebeldom, brought off near 800 slaves and thousands of dollars worth of property.

Although she may have wished to go back North to see her parents, Tubman stayed on in South Carolina. She kept working, doing what she could to help the war effort. In the winter of 1863–1864, an acquaintance, the son of abolitionist William Lloyd Garrison, visited the military camp where Tubman was based. He wrote in a letter: "She wants to go North, but says General Gilmore will not let her go. . . . He thinks her services are too valuable to lose. She has made it a business to see all contrabands escaping from the rebels, and is able to get more intelligence than anybody else."

In July 1863, a black regiment, the 54th Massachusetts Volunteer Infantry, led by Colonel Robert Gould Shaw, launched an assault on Fort Wagner in Charleston Harbor. The Union regiment lost badly, and Shaw was killed. To show their contempt for a white man who led black troops, the Confederates threw Shaw's body into a mass grave with his slain men. Shaw is remembered today as a fair and brave man, ahead of his time. Tubman is said to have nursed the many soldiers who were wounded in the assault of Fort Wagner. For her, as for many Americans, this was a very long war.

A Country
Still Divided

After four long years of war, General Robert E. Lee of the Confederate Army and General Ulysses S. Grant of the Union Army met in the parlor of a house in the small town of Appomattox Court House, Virginia. "It would be useless and therefore cruel to provoke the further effusion of blood, and I have arranged to meet with General Grant with a view to surrender," said General Lee on that morning of April 9, 1865. It took just 90 minutes for General Lee to surrender the Confederate Army of Northern Virginia to General Grant. Other Confederate generals surrendered in the following weeks. The Confederate president, Jefferson Davis, was captured in early May.

The long war was over, but the wounds did not heal for some time. The battlefields of the Civil War saw the deaths of 630,000 soldiers from the South and the North. Another million men were wounded. In his famous poem, "The Blue and the Gray," Francis Miles Finch mourned for those lost on both sides:

> *Under the sod and the dew,*
> *Waiting the Judgment Day:*
> *Love and tears for the Blue,*
> *Tears and love for the Gray.*

Within days of Lee's surrender, the United States experienced a shocking loss. President Lincoln had begun his second term in January. With the end of the war, he hoped to reunite the country. Lincoln looked forward to a new era of cooperation, as well as to freedom for all slaves. In a speech on April 11, he said that he believed black soldiers should be given the vote. He did not live to see the changes he wanted to bring about. On Friday, April 14, 1865, President Lincoln attended a play at Ford's Theatre in Washington, D.C. A well-known actor named John Wilkes Booth entered the president's box, aimed a small pistol at the back of Lincoln's head, and fatally shot the president. The assassination was part of a larger conspiracy. That same night, Tubman's old friend from Auburn, William Seward, who was Lincoln's secretary of state, also was attacked. Unlike Lincoln, Seward survived.

The postwar years were difficult for many Americans. Southern states faced economic ruin. Entire cities, such as Atlanta, Georgia, had been burned by Union armies. All through the South, bridges and roads were destroyed. In the countryside, houses and farm buildings lay in rubble. People scrounged desperately for food. In many families, fathers and sons were dead.

Tens of thousands of former slaves also had to find their way in a new, uncertain world. For a brief time, Tubman stayed in the South. She wanted to give freed slaves something that she had never had: an education. She helped to raise money

It was illegal to teach slaves how to read, and literacy was discouraged even in small free black communities. After the war, schools for freed people opened and were overflowing with newly freed slaves eager to learn. Within a year of freedom, at least 8,000 former slaves were attending schools in Georgia; within eight years, nearly 20,000 blacks had enrolled in Georgian schools. Pictured is a school for freed slaves in 1870.

for schools and hospitals for newly free men and women. Harriet also worked at Fort Monroe, the federal compound in Hampton, Virginia. There, she nursed wounded soldiers who were waiting to return home.

A TRAIN RIDE

Although the war was over, freedom for African Americans was still just a promise. On her way back to her parents and friends in Auburn, New York, Tubman boarded a train in Philadelphia. The train was segregated, as trains in much of the South would be for another 100 years. As the train rumbled into New

Jersey, the conductor told Tubman to move from her seat. The conductor did not believe her papers, which said that she had served the Union Army. Tubman refused to get up, and the conductor lost his temper. He grabbed her and cursed at her. As Tubman fought to get away, several other passengers rose to help the conductor. Tubman held onto a railing as the group tried to pull her away. In the struggle, her arm may have been broken. When her assailants finally threw her into the baggage car, she suffered more injuries. White passengers shouted at her and urged that she be put off the train.

In 1863, when President Lincoln delivered his great address after the Battle of Gettysburg, he said that the war was about "a

THE RIGHT TO VOTE

Even after the Fifteenth Amendment was passed, in 1870, black men struggled for the right to cast ballots in elections. Although the amendment prohibited discrimination on the basis of race, color, or previous slavery, black men still faced barriers to voting, particularly in the South. Many Southern states wrote provisions into their state constitutions that made it difficult, if not impossible, for black men and even poor white men to vote. Literacy tests required people to show that they know how to read before they could vote. Poll taxes demanded payment to vote. Black voters also were turned away from the polls through the use of violence and through so-called Jim Crow laws that separated the races in public places such as schools and courthouses. Voting restrictions were a signal that, although slavery was now history, America's African-American citizens were still denied many basic civil rights. Tubman knew this all too well.

new birth of freedom." Now, the North had won the war, but Tubman saw that freedom was a long way off. Slavery had not been fully abolished. In Kentucky, for example, there still were 40,000 slaves. Because the Emancipation Proclamation applied only to the states of the former Confederacy, several other slave states that had stayed loyal to the Union had not yet outlawed slavery. To accomplish that, a Constitutional amendment was needed. The Constitution already had 12 amendments, many of which related to civil rights. The First Amendment, for example, protected free speech.

After debate in the House, in the Senate, and in state legis-latures, the Thirteenth Amendment was adopted on December 6, 1865. Two-thirds of the 36 states had ratified it. The amend-ment states: "Neither slavery nor involuntary servitude . . . shall exist within the United States." Two more important amend-ments relating to the rights and liberties of black citizens soon followed. The Fourteenth Amendment, adopted in 1868, states that all people born or naturalized in the United States are citizens and have the right to due process of law. The Fifteenth Amendment, adopted in 1870, gave African-American men the right to vote. For many freed slaves, however, life was still a struggle. They did not have the land, the money, or the skills that they needed to become self-sufficient and care for their families. Many freed slaves still worked for little or no pay under their former masters.

WOMEN'S RIGHTS

Tubman came home to Auburn to begin a new chapter of her life. As in her earlier years, Tubman's later life was devoted to others. She used her growing fame to raise money to build hospitals and schools in the South to serve freed men and women. She also aided people in her own community. Tubman always believed that she was called by God to help her people. "Now do you suppose he wanted me to do this just for a day, or a week? No! The Lord who told me to take care of my people meant me to do it just so long as I live, and so I do what he told me to do," she once said. She continued to beat the drum for equal rights.

For Tubman, equal rights applied not only to the races, but also to the sexes. With the end of slavery, black women, as well as white women, still lacked many of the basic rights given to black and white men. Upstate New York was a center for the women's rights movement. The campaign for equal rights and freedom for women took off in 1848, at the first Women's Rights Convention in Seneca Falls, New York, not far from Tubman's home in Auburn. At that convention, Elizabeth Cady Stanton, one of the founders of the movement, laid out a Declaration of Sentiments and a list of 12 resolutions. The resolutions listed such grievances as women not being allowed to attend college, own property, or enter professions such as the law and medicine. The most controversial issue was women's suffrage—the right of women to vote. In 1848, the goal seemed so unattainable that the women at the convention could not agree that the time was right. Someone once asked Tubman whether she believed that women should vote. Her response was, "I suffered enough to believe it." The Nineteenth Amendment to the Constitution, which gave American women the right to vote, was not ratified until 1920, after Tubman's death.

Tubman's belief in the equality of all people made her sympathetic to the women's movement. She knew some of its leaders, many of whom had been prominent abolitionists. Susan B. Anthony, for example, had conducted an antislavery campaign in upstate New York in 1861 with the slogan, "No Union with Slaveholders. No Compromise." Tubman's friend Lucretia Mott, whom she had met in Philadelphia soon after her escape from slavery, was another strong advocate for women's rights.

Tubman traveled to women's suffrage meetings in Washington, D.C., New York, and Boston. She was treated

In her later years, Tubman worked alongside activists Susan B. Anthony *(standing)* and Elizabeth Cady Stanton *(left)* for a woman's right to vote. Traveling to major cities to tell her story during and after the Civil War, she also spoke on the countless sacrifices made by women throughout history as an example of women's equality with men. Anthony and Stanton took on prominent roles in the anti-slavery movement.

with great respect and honored for her achievements. She was especially interested in the rights of African-American women. In 1896, she was invited to speak at the first meeting of the National Association of Colored Women. Her reputation as a public speaker—an orator—had begun before the war, when she gave antislavery speeches. Now, she was invited to give speeches about women's rights.

Despite never having learned to read or write, Tubman was a spellbinding and popular speaker. She told stories and parables, often based on passages in the Bible. She used the language and sayings of her youth as a field worker in Maryland. People listened to her every word. Often, she wove stories of her years in slavery into her speeches and spoke about her work as a nurse during the war. Historian Albert Bushnell Hart records the following words from a Tubman speech: "And then we saw the lightening, and that was the guns; and then we heard the thunder, and that was the big guns; and then we heard the rain falling, and that was the drops of blood falling." She also told funny stories that made her audiences laugh.

In October 1865, Harriet visited a church in Brooklyn, New York. She spoke to a large audience about her slave experiences. The audience was enthralled. "Her master was a good man, but she knew that God had directed her to perform other works in this world, and so she escaped from bondage. . . . Her narration of her sickness, previous to her escape, was filled with negro phrases and elicited shouts of laughter from this congregation, the whites entering most heartily into it," wrote a reporter for *The Brooklyn Eagle*.

A SECOND MARRIAGE

In 1867, Tubman heard tragic news from back home in Maryland. Her former husband, John, had been killed that September by a white man named Robert Vincent. The two men had an argument, and it turned violent. The white man was arrested and tried in court, but he was not convicted. In the 1860s, to find a jury willing to consider convicting a white man accused of killing a black man was not very likely.

In 1869, Tubman married for a second time. She was in her late forties, and her new husband was only about 25 years old. Nelson Charles Davis was a tall man; he stood nearly a foot above Tubman. He was a brickmaker who had escaped from slavery in North Carolina and served as a soldier in a black regiment during the Civil War.

Tubman sometimes called Davis "the soldier." She met him when he lived as a boarder in her house. Unlike her first marriage, which was not legal because she was a slave and probably was not marked by a ceremony, this wedding was celebrated as a big event. The marriage took place on March 18, 1869, at the Central Presbyterian Church in Auburn. Many of Tubman's friends and neighbors came to the wedding. In 1874, the couple adopted a baby girl named Gertie. The child joined a large household that included several relatives and people down on their luck who needed a place to stay. Tubman and Davis worked a small farm to make ends meet. Tubman raised pigs, chickens, and a few cows and sold eggs and milk. Although Davis was much younger than Tubman, she outlived him. He died in 1888, when he was about 45 years old, probably from tuberculosis.

A MILITARY PENSION

Even as she raised money for others, Tubman struggled to pay for her own food and clothing. Two years after Davis died, the federal government began to give pensions to the widows of Civil War soldiers. Finally, Tubman received a monthly check from the government, not for her own service, but for her husband's. Most widows received only $8 every month. After Tubman's supporters wrote to Congress about her years of service, however, her check was raised to $20. This still was not enough for her to live on. Struggling to pay for necessities on this small pension made her life very difficult.

Tubman's wartime service was informal and was not well documented. She believed, however, that it was an injustice that she did not receive a pension of her own. Tubman began to fight for what she felt was hers. She turned to her longtime friend William Seward, who had served in the Lincoln administration. He wrote the following letter to General David Hunter:

Washington, July 25, 1865
Maj. Gen. Hunter—

MY DEAR SIR: Harriet Tubman, a colored woman, has been nursing our soldiers during nearly all the War. She believes she has a claim for faithful services to the command in South Carolina with which you are connected, and she thinks that you would be disposed to see her claim justly settled.

I have known her long, and a nobler, higher spirit, or truer, seldom dwells in the human form. I commend her, therefore, to your kind and best attentions.

Faithfully your friend,
William H. Seward

General Hunter could not help her. Seward asked Congress several times, but he was unable to secure a promise.

Tubman decided to make some money by telling the story of her life. A publisher offered to print the book, and her friends pitched in with funding. She began to tell her story to Sarah Bradford, a white schoolteacher, writer, and abolitionist. In Bradford's book, *Scenes in the Life of Harriet Tubman*, Tubman spoke about her hard childhood in slavery, her rescues on the Underground Railroad, and her work during the Civil War. Bradford wrote to Tubman's acquaintances and included their praises in the book. The Boston abolitionist, lawyer, and speaker Wendell Phillips wrote this: "In my opinion there are few captains, perhaps few colonels, who have done more for the loyal cause since the war began, and few men who did before that time more for the colored race, than our fearless and most sagacious friend, Harriet." Bradford's book was published in 1869. A revised version of the book appeared in 1886.

A HOME FOR OTHERS

Tubman's brothers and their families eventually settled around Auburn. Nieces and nephews also lived nearby. Tubman's parents passed away during these years. Her father died in about 1871; her mother died in 1880. Tubman always kept her door open to people who needed shelter and food. During the course of many years, freed slaves came and went in her house on South Street, on the outskirts of Auburn. Tubman's guests were fed and cared for until they were able to move on. She showed special concern for elderly African-American men and women who struggled to live on their own. The freed slaves had little money, or even homes of their own, to sustain them during their old age. There were few social services for any citizens, and fewer still for former slaves who were too old or ill to earn a living. Tubman looked for a way to help those in need in her community.

In 1896, Tubman went to an auction to bid for 25 acres of land next to her property. "They were all white folks there but me, and I was there like a blackberry in a pail of milk," she later said. Despite having only a small amount of money, Tubman was able to place the winning bid. She could not pay for the land by herself, but a local bank and her church helped her out. She was unable to meet the taxes on the land, however. One year, she had to sell some of her cows to pay the tax bill. In 1903, she deeded the property to her church, the Thompson Memorial A.M.E. Zion Church, because she could not afford it any longer.

Tubman continued her work in aiding the poor and aged by opening the Harriet Tubman Home for the Aged (*above*), in Auburn, New York. Built in 1908 to shelter aged and indigent African Americans, Tubman herself was cared for here when her own health deteriorated. Today her three properties—the Home for the Aged, the Thompson AME Zion Church, and the Harriet Tubman Residence—are recognized as a National Historic Landmark.

In 1908, Tubman finally achieved a dream. She opened a home for the elderly in a white clapboard house on her property. In late June, at the opening ceremony, she wore a long gown, a knee-length cape, and "her favorite small brim hat," according to a local newspaper. The home was known as the Harriet Tubman Home for Aged and Indigent Negroes.

Tubman still suffered from the headaches that began when she was hit on the head as a young teen. Although her mind was very clear, she fell asleep in the middle of conversations.

At long last, she sought medical attention. One day in the late 1890s, as she was walking in Boston, she passed Massachusetts General Hospital. As she later told her friend Samuel Hopkins, "So I went right in, and I saw a young man there, and I said, "Sir, are you a doctor?" It was decided that she needed surgery. The doctor shaved her head, and the operation proceeded without anesthesia. Tubman bit a bullet to help her stand the pain. Once again, Tubman's stubborn determination helped her to accomplish what might seem impossible for an ordinary person.

The Moses
of Her People

By 1911, Tubman was entering her nineties. She had to use a wheelchair. Aunt Harriet—as she was known to friends, family, and the entire community—could no longer live on her own. With the help of friends, she moved into the Harriet Tubman Home. She was unable to pay the costs, however. Several newspapers ran articles about her and asked for donations. On June 2, 1911, the *New York Times* ran a short article: "Harriet Tubman, the aged negro woman, who piloted more than 400 slaves to freedom prior to the civil war and who was befriended by Lincoln, Seward, Garrison, Wendell Phillips, and John Brown was today taken to the Harriet Tubman home penniless." Fortunately, people stepped in to help the woman they so admired. Her last years were peaceful ones. She lived comfortably, surrounded by friends and relatives.

After a life that stretched across a turbulent American century, Tubman died of pneumonia on March 10, 1913, in Auburn. Throughout her many years, she always had tried to help others. By some accounts, her last words were as generous as her life, "I go to prepare a place for you." A service was held at the Harriet Tubman Home. Her body then lay in state at her longtime place of worship, the Thompson Memorial A.M.E. Zion Church. Years earlier, Tubman had helped to raise funds to construct the church building, and the church congregation had always been there to help her.

Hundreds of people came to the church to honor Tubman and her life of service. Newspapers sent reporters to cover Tubman's farewell. According to one report, as she lay in state, she wore the Diamond Jubilee medal that had been sent to her by Britain's Queen Victoria. A reporter for the *Auburn Daily Advertiser* wrote a story entitled "Aunt Harriet's Funeral." At the memorial, the president of the Auburn city council said this:

> It is appropriate that the city give official recognition of the passing of this wonderful woman. No one of our fellow citizens of late years has conferred greater distinction upon us than has she. I can say that I have known "Aunt Harriet" during my whole lifetime. The boys of my time always regarded her as a sort of supernatural being; our youthful imaginations were fired by the tales we had heard of her adventures and we stood in great awe of her. We came to believe she was all-wise.

Because of her service in the Civil War, Tubman was given military honors at her funeral by an Auburn representative of the Grand Army of the Republic—the Union Army. Her obituary ran in the *New York Times* and other newspapers across the nation.

Tubman was buried at Fort Hill Cemetery in Auburn. She was laid to rest next to her brother, William Henry Stewart,

Sr., and his son and daughter-in-law. Tubman's second husband, Nelson Davis, is also buried in the cemetery. In 1914, the citizens of Auburn unveiled a plaque that is now on the Cayuga County Courthouse. The plaque says, in part: "She braved every danger and overcome every obstacle, withal she possessed extraordinary foresight and judgment so that she truthfully said—'On my Underground Railroad I nebber run my train off de track.'"

HONORS COME LATER

Recognition of Tubman's many achievements grew as more people became interested in the history of slavery and of African Americans. In 1937, the Empire State Federation of Women's Clubs paid for a monument to mark Tubman's grave. "Servant of God, Well Done" are the words on the granite monument. "Women at Auburn Honor 'Aunt Harriet' of Underground Railroad," stated the *New York Times*.

Other honors followed. During World War II, a Liberty ship was named for Harriet Tubman. Tubman also was featured on several U.S. postage stamps, including one in 1978 and another in 1995. The brick house where Tubman lived and the white clapboard house that housed the Harriet Tubman Home are now part of the Harriet Tubman National Historic Site in Auburn. Visitors to the site can learn much about Tubman's life and work. All across the United States, students study in public schools named for Tubman. These include the Harriet Tubman School, also P.S. 154, on West 127th Street in New York City, and the Harriet Tubman High School in Compton, California. Every year, new efforts are made to celebrate Tubman. In 2005, a statue of "Nana Tubman" was unveiled in the city of Aburi, in Ghana, the West African homeland of Tubman's ancestors. Halfway across the world, in 2007, a section of Fulton Street, a major thoroughfare in Brooklyn, New York, was co-named in Tubman's honor.

After Harriet Tubman bought her home, she had trouble paying the taxes. Once she had to sell off her cows for money. Located on 26 acres, the Harriet Tubman Home was abandoned for many years prior to its restoration in 1953. Today, it is a museum and education center that offers tours to visitors and special events are held each Memorial Day weekend.

In 1990, Congress passed a law making March 10 the anniversary of her death, Harriet Tubman Day. In 2003, New York governor George E. Pataki established March 10 as Harriet Tubman Day in New York State. Every year on that day, the Harriet Tubman Home in Auburn, New York, hosts a celebration of her life. In 2008, the Genesee African Dancers from the after-school program of the local elementary school performed dances in Tubman's honor. A woman read passages from a Tubman biography. Guest speakers spoke about how Tubman influenced their lives. "I hope everyone learned a little bit about

Harriet Tubman today," said one speaker. "She was not only a great abolitionist; she was brave enough to say something that was dangerous to say at the time."

BACK PAY

Tubman never received full payment for her courageous service as a nurse, spy, and scout during the Civil War. In 2000, New York congressman Edolphus Towns introduced a bill in the U.S. Congress to grant Tubman the veteran status she was denied during her lifetime. The fact that she had received no pay still outraged many members of Tubman's family and others seeking to keep her memory alive. In 2003, Ward DeWitt, executive director of the Harriet Tubman Home, said this to the *New York Times*: "She has never gotten a pension for her service as a scout or a spy, her actual military service. It's an obligation, I think, of the United States."

In 2002, a teacher at the Albany Free School in Albany, New York, took his class to visit the Harriet Tubman Home. The seventh- and eighth-grade students had studied Tubman's life and considered her a great hero. At the home, they learned about her lost pension and about how she had to struggle financially for so long. "They were outraged that she had been stiffed by the government," the teacher, Chris Mercogliano, told the *New York Times*. The class decided to do something about the injustice. They wrote a letter to their U.S. senator, Hillary Clinton. "We do not think it's fair that she wasn't paid," eighth-grader Holley Newell told the *Albany Times-Union*, a local newspaper.

Later, the students took a two-week trip to follow the escape route of Tubman from Maryland to Philadelphia. They also met with Senator Clinton in Washington, D.C. Thanks to the students' efforts, in 2003, the Senate included $11,750 in an appropriations bill to help maintain the Harriet Tubman Home. Senator Clinton said in a statement:

I thank the Albany students who brought this matter to my attention last year and I am proud that we can now honor the memory of Harriet Tubman by making sure that this injustice is remedied. Harriet Tubman was one of our nation's most courageous freedom fighters. It is important that we officially recognize her extraordinary service.

The money represented part, but not all, of Tubman's lost pension. As the *New York Times* reported, the total amount she was due was close to $210,000 in 2003 dollars.

DISPELLING MYTHS

Several biographies of Tubman were written during her lifetime and in the early twentieth century. Starting in the 1940s, many children's books were published that told about Tubman and the Underground Railroad. Her heroic story shed light on such important issues as slavery, the Underground Railroad, and the Civil War. The award-winning picture book *Moses: When Harriet Tubman Led her People to Freedom*, written by Carole Boston Weatherford and illustrated by Kadir Nelson, focused on Tubman's strong religious faith. Other books focused on her bravery in the face of danger. Learning about Tubman helped young people to become familiar with the life-and-death struggles of slaves and to learn to examine the injustices that still exist in today's world. Because at the time of the books' writing, many details of Tubman's life remained unknown, the books may have simplified her history. Not all of the books were historically accurate, and in some of them, some of Tubman's achievements were exaggerated. For example, Tubman's first biographer wrote that she had saved 300 people from slavery. Later researchers found a lower number. In short, the real Harriet Tubman still awaited discovery.

As the years went by, interest grew in the Underground Railroad and in the roles played by freed and enslaved blacks in the fight against slavery in the years before the Civil War. People wanted to find the flesh-and-blood person behind the mythical Tubman. Not surprisingly, the woman they discovered was even more interesting and admirable than the one previously imagined.

HARRIET'S PAINTER

The African-American painter Jacob Lawrence heard about Tubman from his mother, teachers, and librarians when he was a teenager in New York City's Harlem. Lawrence was born in Atlantic City, New Jersey, in 1917. At the age of 13, he and his family moved to Harlem. There, he was surrounded by the art, poetry, and music of the African-American cultural revival known as the Harlem Renaissance. He attended after-school art classes at a community center, where he made masks and met the painter Charles Alsop, who encouraged him as an artist.

When the Great Depression brought hard times, and his mother lost her job, Lawrence kept on painting. He attended workshops and found space to work in other artists' studios. He had only cheap paint and paper with which to work. Despite these limitations, Lawrence painted with the bold colors and simple lines that later made him famous.

Lawrence was part of an art movement known as social realism, which focused on the realities of life for people who were poor or working class. Lawrence painted the struggles and joys of people on city streets. At the urging of his teachers, he began reading about the African-American experience. He wanted to use his art to tell little-known stories of courage, and a single painting often

In 2003, historian Kate Clifford Larson published a scholarly biography of Tubman called *Bound for the Promised Land*. Larson's research exemplified the new effort to examine Tubman's life in all its rich complexity. Larson dug through slave records in Maryland, old newspapers, letters, and journals.

was not enough. In 1939, after researching Tubman's life, Lawrence painted 31 panels showing her journey from slave child to conductor on the Underground Railroad. He used tempera paints in deep, brilliant colors and applied his paint in bold, clean strokes. The paintings later were published in a children's book, *Harriet and the Promised Land*.

Lawrence also created a series of paintings about Frederick Douglass, a series about John Brown, and a series about Toussaint L'Ouverture, a freed slave who led a slave rebellion in Haiti. In 1941, the 24-year-old Lawrence earned widespread recognition with a series of 60 paintings called The Migration of the Negro. The series depicts the movement of more than one million African Americans from the rural South to cities such as Chicago and New York during the years from 1910 to 1940.

Lawrence became the most famous African-American artist in the United States. Together with his wife, the artist Gwendolyn Knight, he continued to paint the African-American experience and to teach art to young students until his death in 2000. To his biographer Ellen Harkins Wheat, Lawrence said this: "If at times my productions do not express the conventionally beautiful, there is always an effort to express the universal beauty of man's continuous struggle to lift his social position and to add dimension to his spiritual being."

Tubman became an icon in the years after her death. This statue of Tubman is in Aburi, Ghana, where it is believed the Tubman clan is descended. There have been many other honors, including the first ship named for a black woman, christened the SS *Harriet Tubman*, the naming of dozens of schools, the issuing of a postage stamp with her image, and numerous statues and sculptures.

Other modern historians and biographers also have probed deeply into Tubman's life and times. Jean Humez published *Harriet Tubman: The Life and Life Stories* in 2003; and Catherine Clinton published *Harriet Tubman: The Road to Freedom* in 2004. Taken together, these three books based on primary sources and modern research have shone a clearer light on Tubman.

"A GLORY OVER EVERYTHING"

When Harriet Tubman crossed the Pennsylvania border in 1849 and took her first breath of freedom, she was all alone in a strange land. She left behind a life of hardship and humiliation, and she had no idea what lay ahead. She knew only that freedom was better than slavery. Her childhood had been one of deprivation, hard labor, unreasonable punishment, and physical pain. Those experiences helped push her to leave her family and loved ones behind and give up everything in the pursuit of freedom.

It was not only her difficult past that led Tubman to escape from slavery, however. It was also her hoped-for future, which pulled her toward a richer, fuller life. Her strong religious faith gave her the belief that something better was waiting for her. Throughout Tubman's life, whether she was leading slaves away to freedom, opening her home to the poor, or championing the rights of women, she never took that first breath of freedom for granted. She always tried to strengthen the freedom of others. It might have been because Tubman never forgot that fresh sense of relief and joy when she first crossed over the Mason Dixon line.

As Tubman told Sarah Bradford, "I looked at my hands, to see if I was the same person now that I was free. There was such a glory over everything, the sun came like gold through the trees, and over the fields, and I felt like I was in heaven."

CHRONOLOGY

c. 1820 Araminta "Minty" Ross, later known as Harriet Tubman, is born in Dorchester County, Maryland.

1825 Tubman's owner, Edward Brodess, hires her out to work.

(approx.) 1835-1837 Tubman is hit on the head by a heavy weight thrown by an overseer who is chasing a runaway slave.

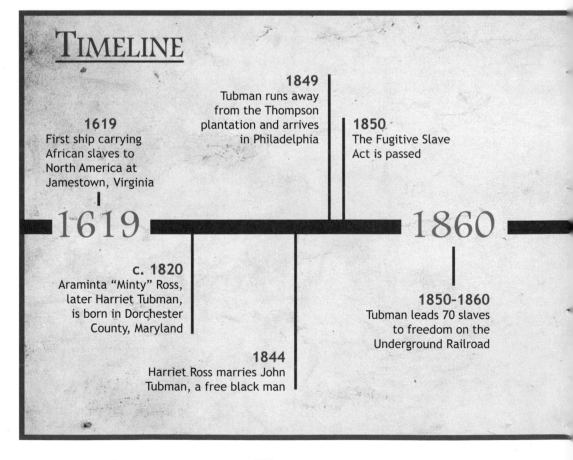

TIMELINE

1619
First ship carrying African slaves to North America at Jamestown, Virginia

1849
Tubman runs away from the Thompson plantation and arrives in Philadelphia

1850
The Fugitive Slave Act is passed

1619

1860

c. 1820
Araminta "Minty" Ross, later Harriet Tubman, is born in Dorchester County, Maryland

1844
Harriet Ross marries John Tubman, a free black man

1850-1860
Tubman leads 70 slaves to freedom on the Underground Railroad

1844   Araminta Ross marries John Tubman, a free black man.

1847-1849   Tubman is hired out to Anthony Thompson and works as a field hand.

1849   Tubman runs away from Anthony Thompson's plantation in Maryland and arrives in Philadelphia.

1850-1860   Tubman leads 70 slaves to freedom on the Underground Railroad.

1857   Tubman rescues her parents from Maryland and takes them to Canada.

1861
President Abraham Lincoln takes office. The Civil War begins

1863
Emancipation Proclamation frees slaves in the Confederate states

1908
The Harriet Tubman Home for Aged and Indigent Negroes opens in Auburn, New York

1869
Tubman marries Civil War veteran Nelson Davis

1861 ———————— **1913**

1863
In June, Harriet leads a raid up the Combahee River in South Carolina; the raid frees 700 to 800 slaves

1865
The Civil War ends; President Lincoln is assassinated. The Thirteenth Amendment to the Constitution outlaws slavery

1913
Tubman dies of pneumonia on March 10

1859	Tubman and her parents move to Auburn, New York.
1861	President Abraham Lincoln takes office. The Civil War begins.
1862	Tubman travels to Port Royal, South Carolina, to help the war effort.
1863	In June, Tubman leads a raid with Colonel James Montgomery up the Combahee River in South Carolina; the raid frees 700 to 800 slaves.
1865	The Civil War ends. President Lincoln is assassinated. The Thirteenth Amendment to the Constitution outlaws slavery.
1869	Tubman marries Civil War veteran Nelson Davis.
1908	The Harriet Tubman Home for Aged and Indigent Negroes opens in Auburn, New York.
1913	Tubman dies of pneumonia on March 10.

GLOSSARY

abolition   The movement to end and prohibit slavery.

civil rights   The rights people have to justice and freedom, regardless of race, sex, or religion.

Confederacy   The 11 Southern states that seceded, or withdrew, from the United States and became the Confederate States of America.

conductor   A person, such as Harriet Tubman, who aided runaway slaves (called "passengers") on the Underground Railroad.

emancipation   Freedom from slavery.

fugitive slave   A slave who flees from his or her owner.

irony   A clever literary form in which a writer uses words to say the opposite of what the writer really means.

orator   A person who is skilled at giving public speeches.

secede   To withdraw, or separate, as the Southern states withdrew from the Union.

spiritual   A traditional religious song sung by African-American slaves.

Underground Railroad   A secret network of people who helped slaves to escape from slave-holding states to the free states of the North or to Canada.

Union   The Northern states that stayed loyal to the federal government during the American Civil War.

✂ BIBLIOGRAPHY ✂

Adler, Margot. "Douglass Memorial Sparks Debate on Art vs. History." *All Things Considered*, March 5, 2007. Available online at http://www.npr.org/templates/story/story.php?story Id=7685316.

Bibb, Henry. *Narrative of the Life and Adventures of Henry Bibb*, Electronic edition. Available online at http://docsouth.unc.edu/ neh/bibb/bibb.html.

Blight, David W. *Passages to Freedom: The Underground Railroad in History and Memory*. New York: Smithsonian Institution/ HarperCollins, 2004.

Bordewich, Fergus M. *Bound for Canaan: The Underground Railroad and the War for the Soul of America*. New York: Amistad, 2005.

Bradford, Sarah H. *Scenes in the Life of Harriet Tubman*. Auburn, N.Y.: W.J. Moses, 1869. Available online at http://docsouth.unc. edu/neh/bradford/menu.html.

———. *Harriet: The Moses of Her People*. New York: Geo. R. Lockwood & Son, 1886. Available online at http://docsouth. unc.edu/neh/harriet/harriet.html.

Clinton, Catherine. *Harriet Tubman: The Road to Freedom*. New York: Little, Brown and Company, 2004.

Conrad, Earl. *Harriet Tubman*. Washington, D.C.: Associated Publishers, 1943.

"Dred Scott's Fight for Freedom," *Africans in America*, PBS. Available online at http://www.pbs.org/wgbh/aia/ part4/4p2932.html.

Following the Freedom Trail in Auburn and Cayuga County, New York. Available online at http://www.auburncayuga freedomtrail.com/.

Fricano, Mike. "Students feel slaves' fearful flight." *Albany Times-Union*, May 15, 2002. Available online at http://www. albanyfreeschool.com/press_tu.shtml.

Gabak, Jason. "Harriet Tubman's life honored." *The Citizen*, March 11, 2008. Available online at http://www.auburnpub. com/articles/2008/03/11/latest_news/latestnews03.txt.

"Harriet Tubman Dying." The *New York Times*, March 11, 1911. Available online at http://query.nytimes.com/mem/archive-free/ pdf?res=9C03E2DE1F3AE633A25752C1A9659C946296D6CF.

"Harriet Tubman Penniless." The *New York Times*, June 2, 1911. Available online at http://query.nytimes.com/mem/archive-free/pdf?_r=1&res=9E02E4D91431E233A25751C0A9609C9 46096D6CF&oref=slogin.

"Harriet Tubman, the Colored Nurse and Scout." *Brooklyn Eagle*, October 23, 1865. Available online at http://eagle.brooklyn publiclibrary.org/Repository/getFiles.asp?Style=OliveXLib: ArticleToMailGifMSIE&Type=text/html&Path=BEG/1865/10/ 23&ID=Ar00207&Locale=&ChunkNum=0.

Harriet Tubman Special Resource Study, National Park Service, U.S. Department of the Interior. Available online at http://www. harriettubmanstudy.org/.

Harriet Tubman Historical Society. Available online at http:// www.harriettubman.com/index.html.

Humez, Jean M. *Harriet Tubman The Life and the Life Stories*. Madison, Wisconsin: The University of Wisconsin Press, 2003.

"John Brown," *Africans in America*, PBS. Available online at http://www.pbs.org/wgbh/aia/part4/4p1550.html.

Larson, Kate Clifford. *Bound for the Promised Land: Harriet Tubman, Portrait of an American Hero*. New York: Ballantine Books, 2003.

Quarles, Benjamin. *The Negro in the Civil War*. New York: De Capo Press, 1987.

Slackman, Michael. "In Search of Back Pay for Heroine of Civil War." The *New York Times*, November 1, 2003, B1.

Stukin, Stacie. "Unravelling the Myth of Quilts and the Underground Railroad." *Time* magazine, April 3, 2007. Available online at http://www.time.com/time/arts/article/0,8599, 1606271,00.html.

"Sweet Chariot: The Story of the Spirituals." The Spirituals Project at the University of Denver. Available online at http://ctl.du.edu/spirituals/Freedom/source.cfm.

The Harriet Tubman Journal. Available online at http://www.harriettubmanjournal.com/index.html.

FURTHER RESOURCES

BOOKS

Ayres, Katherine. *North by Night: A Story of the Underground Railroad*. New York: Yearling Books, 2000.

Carson, Mary Kay. *The Underground Railroad for Kids: From Slavery to Freedom with 21 Activities*. Chicago: Chicago Review Press, 2005.

Devillers, David. *The John Brown Slavery Revolt Trial: A Headline Court Case*. Springfield, N.J.: Enslow Publishers, 2000.

Freedman, Russell. *Lincoln: A Photobiography*. New York: Clarion, 1987.

Hansen, Joyce, and McGowan, Gary. *Freedom Roads: Searching for the Underground Railroad*. Peterborough, N.H.: Cricket Books, 2005.

Katz, William Loren. *Breaking the Chains: African American Slave Resistance*. New York: Atheneum, 1990.

Lester, Julius. *To Be a Slave*. New York: Puffin, 2000.

Lowry, Beverly. *Harriet Tubman: Imagining a Life*. New York: Doubleday, 2007.

Paulsen, Gary. *Sarny: A Life Remembered*. New York: Delacorte Books for Young Readers, 1997.

Pickney, Andrea Davis. *Silent Thunder: A Civil War Story*. New York: Hyperion, 1999.

Taylor, Yuval, editor. *Growing Up in Slavery: Stories of Young Slaves as Told by Themselves*. Chicago: Chicago Review Press, 2007.

WEB SITES

American Slave Narratives: An Online Anthology,
    The University of Virginia
    http://xroads.virginia.edu/~hyper/wpa/wpahome.html

The Harriet Tubman Home
    http://www.nyhistory.com/harriettubman/

National Geographic: The Underground Railroad
    http://www.nationalgeographic.com/railroad/j1.html

National Park Service Guide to the Underground Railroad
    http://www.nps.gov/history/ugrr

Pathways to Freedom. Maryland and the Underground Railroad
    http://pathways.thinkport.org/following/

Slavery and the Making of America, PBS: Historical Fiction:
    From the Journal of Hannah Smalls
    http://www.pbs.org/wnet/slavery/teachers/readings2.html

Underground Railroad Living Museum
    http://www.the-ugrr.org/

⚔ PICTURE CREDITS ⚔

INDEX

ABOUT THE AUTHOR

Author **ANN MALASPINA** is a former newspaper reporter who has been writing nonfiction books for young people since 1998. She has a B.A. in English from Kenyon College and an M.S. in journalism from Boston University. Malaspina has written frequently about civil rights and social issues. As she researched Harriet Tubman, she discovered that thousands of fugitive slaves traveled through her home state of New Jersey on their way to New York and Canada. Free black communities such as Springtown and Marshalltown in southern New Jersey were important links on the Underground Railroad. Fugitive slaves then headed to Jersey City, where they evaded slave hunters to board ferries and coal barges across the Hudson River to New York City. From there, they took night trains north to Syracuse and Rochester.